52 Bible Lessons

by

Susan Addington

illustrated by

Janet Armbrust

Cover by Janet Armbrust

ISBN No. 0-382-30485-3

Standardized Subject Code TA ac

Printing No. 98765432

Shining Star Publications
1204 Buchanan St., Box 299
Carthage, IL 62321-0299

Unless otherwise indicated, the New International Version of the Bible was used in preparing the activities in this book.

To the Teacher/Parent

The lessons in this book are divided into four general themes.

Fall: I need God for daily protection and for forgiveness of sins.

Winter: As I celebrate Jesus, my love for Him overflows into helping others.

Spring: Jesus gives me new life through His death and resurrection.

Summer: I want to be more like Jesus, my Creator.

The lessons are interchangeable with various holidays, as noted on the lesson pages. Each lesson includes the following parts:

Timely Truth or **Godly Goal**

Have the children learn these practical ideas. Posting these week by week is recommended.

Bible Verse

This should be posted every week or copied and sent home for children to memorize.

Bible Activity

Before Class and During Class suggestions are given as well as a list of materials needed.

Personal Plan

This important practical plan gives the children something they can work on during the week.

Musical Moment (not in all lessons)

Print the words on a large piece of paper or on a chalkboard for easy singing.

Puppets are used in several of the lessons. Try these ideas:

- Make simple puppets out of paper plates or from the patterns on pages 95-96.
- If you're using a large shape, reproduce the script and glue it to the back of the puppet.
- Record the script ahead of time with help from your family and add musical effects; then play the tape back in class.
- Make a puppet stage from two spring rods with curtains in a doorway.

SS3845

Table of Contents

Fall

Winter

Spring

Summer

Dedication

I would like to dedicate this book to these Mothers and Grandmothers who have been an example of 2 Timothy 1:5 to my family and me: Lucille Smith, Bonnie Addington, Genevieve Lock, Cora Thornberry, and Phyllis Armin.

Burdens

Timeless Truth

God carries my burdens.

Bible Verse

"Praise be to the Lord, to God our Savior, who daily bears our burdens."

Psalm 68:19

Bible Activity–Practical Lesson

Before Class

Gather these materials:
A globe
Tape
Index cards
Pencils

During Class

Explain to the children that you'd like to have them hold some problems in their hands, but first they need to help you list some of their problems. After each of their problems has been listed, one on each index card, hand out the cards as far as they will go.

Ask for a volunteer who is strong enough to carry all the problems you've just handed out. Ask that person to get down on all fours on the floor and have the other children climb on one by one. Soon the pile of children will crumble.

Then have the children bring all the problems to you. Tape the problems on the globe. (You may want to let the children tape them on the globe.)

Musical Moment

Sing as many verses of "He's Got the Whole World in His Hands" as the children know.

Discussion

Who can hold all the problems of the world in His hands? Let's read Psalm 68:19. What should we do when we think about God holding our problems for us?

Praising God can include listing all the neat things we know about God and thanking Him for them. When we do this, it's easy to realize why He can carry our burdens better than we can.

Digging Deeper

What does Matthew 11:29-30 mean?

Personal Plan

List your burdens and problems on a piece of paper. Beside each one write a characteristic of God that shows He is stronger. Copy Psalm 68:19 and read it every day this week.

Hatred

Timeless Truth

Hating others makes me blind to what my life should be.

Bible Verse

"But whoever hates his brother is in the darkness and walks around in the darkness; he does not know where he is going, because the darkness has blinded him." I John 2:11

Bible Activity–Beans and Bags and Bumps

Before Class

Gather these materials:
A large paper grocery bag for each child
A baggie
Beans
Scissors

During Class

Give each child a baggie and 5 beans.

Explain that all the children will have grocery bags put over their heads so they can't see. Then they must walk around the room trying not to bump into others until the teacher calls, "Stop." Each time a child bumps into someone, both children must drop a bean in their individual baggies. When all five beans are in a child's baggie, he is out of the game, takes the bag off his head, and sits down at the side of the room.

The last child with beans in his hand wins.

(You might want to try the game with more beans.)

Discussion

Was it hard to keep from bumping into other people when you couldn't see?

Did you feel confused when you couldn't see where you were going?

Were you happy to take off the blindfold even if you weren't the winner?

Let's read I John 2:11. According to this verse, what causes us to be blind?

Have you ever been so angry with someone that you just didn't know what to do?

How does hate make you blind?

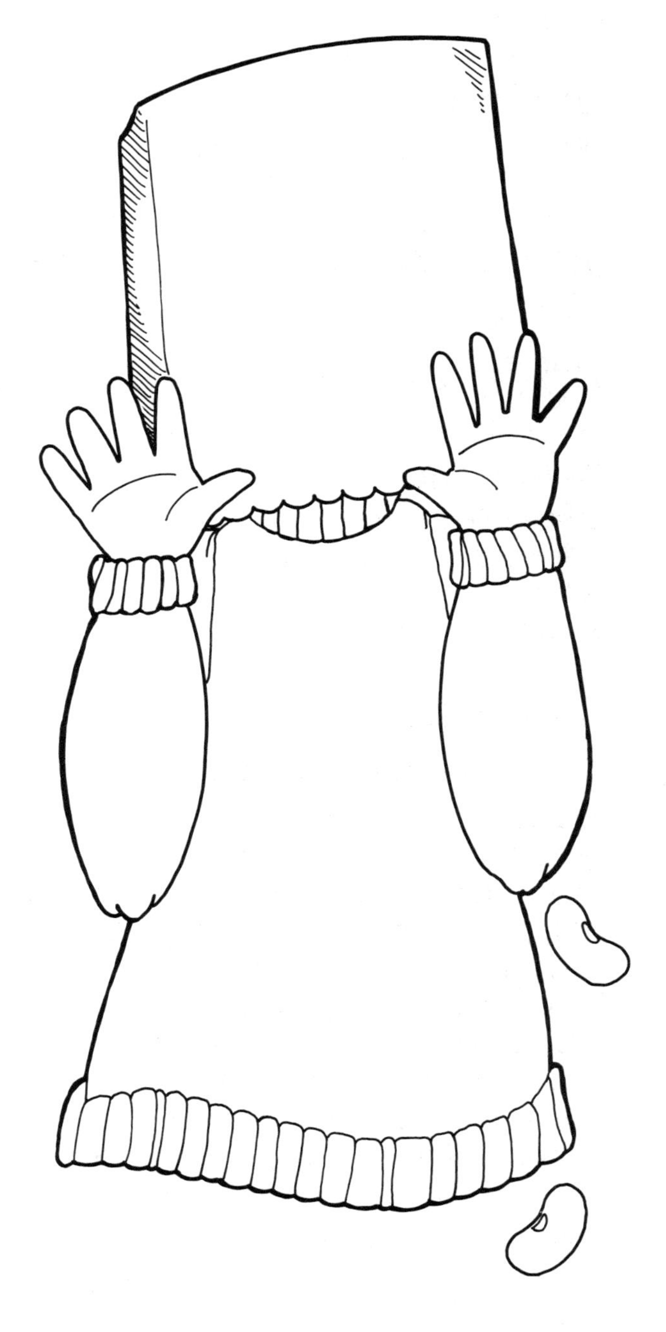

Digging Deeper

Name some Bible characters who hated others.

How did their hate affect their lives?

Personal Plan

Do you hate anyone?

Ask God to help you understand that person the way He does. Copy I John 2:11 and read it over and over this week.

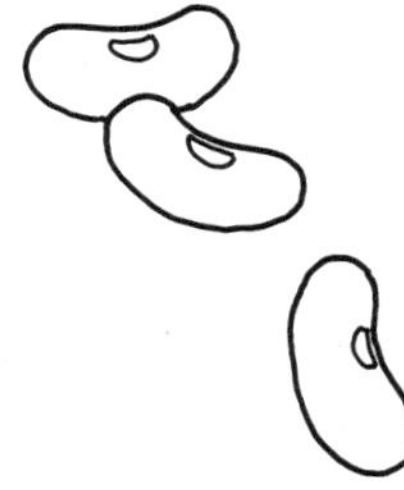

God's Care

Timeless Truth

God's invisible arms surround me.

Bible Verse

"The eternal God is your refuge, and underneath are the everlasting arms."
Deuteronomy 33:27a

Bible Activity–Gliding with God!

Before Class

Gather these materials:
Two paper clips for each child
A plastic straw for each child
Both patterns on this page
Construction paper
Pencil
Scissors

During Class

Demonstrate the construction of the paper glider as follows:

1. Cut out the two patterns and make loops of them.
2. Clip the paper loops to both ends of the straw.
3. Throw the straw like a paper airplane with the small loop in the front. (Check the proportions if the straw doesn't fly smoothly.)

Discussion

Are baby birds afraid when they are learning to fly?

Do bird parents ever send their babies out too early?

What are some things you are afraid to do?

Does God know about your fears?

Let's read Deuteronomy 33:27. How does God help you "glide" through the scary times of life?

Does God ever leave you?

Musical Moment

Sing these words to the tune of "B-I-N-G-O."

My heavenly Father's always near.
He never ever sleeps,
S-L-E-E-P,
S-L-E-E-P,
S-L-E-E-P,
He never, ever sleeps.

My heavenly Father's holding me;
With big, invisible hands,
H-A-N-D-S,
H-A-N-D-S,
H-A-N-D-S,
With big, invisible hands.

Digging Deeper

Who was protected by God's invisible hands in the Bible? When do you need God's invisible hands the most?

Personal Plan

Make a list of some times you have been afraid and everything turned out OK. Thank God for His protection. Copy Deuteronomy 33:27a and read it over and over this week.

Freedom

Timeless Truth
In Christ, I have freedom from sin.

Bible Verse
"It is for freedom that Christ has set us free. Stand firm, then, and do not let yourselves be burdened again by a yoke of slavery." Galatians 5:1

Bible Activity–Window Hanger

Before Class
Gather these materials:
Old red, white, and blue crayons
Gold or silver glitter
Waxed paper
Old pencil sharpener
Star and cross patterns
Scissors
Hole punch
String
Glue
Iron

During Class
Read Galatians 5:1. Talk with the children about the freedom we have because of our country's democratic form of government. Then talk about the freedom Christ provided by His death on the cross. Talk about how to show thankfulness for both.

1. Give each child two pieces of waxed paper.
2. On one sheet of waxed paper, have the children make piles of crayon shavings, keeping the three colors separate. Sprinkle liberal amounts of glitter on top.
3. Lay the second piece of waxed paper on top of the first over the crayon shavings.
4. Place the waxed paper in a sheet of newspaper and place another sheet of newspaper on top. With adult supervision, use a warm iron to melt the crayons and seal the sheets of waxed paper together.
5. When it has cooled, have the children trace two stars and a cross from page 11 onto the waxed paper and cut them out.
6. Use a hole punch to put holes for stringing the patterns together as shown.

Musical Moment

Sing these words to the tune of "He's Got the Whole World in His Hands."

We've got freedom in this land.
We've got freedom in this land.
We've got freedom in this land.
We've got freedom in this land.

We've got freedom in God's Son.
We've got freedom in God's Son.
We've got freedom in God's Son.
We've got freedom in God's Son.

Digging Deeper

What people traveled to a new land like the Pilgrims and settlers in the United States?

Personal Plan

List some reasons you are thankful to live in this country. Then list some reasons you are thankful for Jesus. Copy Galatians 5:1 and read it over and over this week.

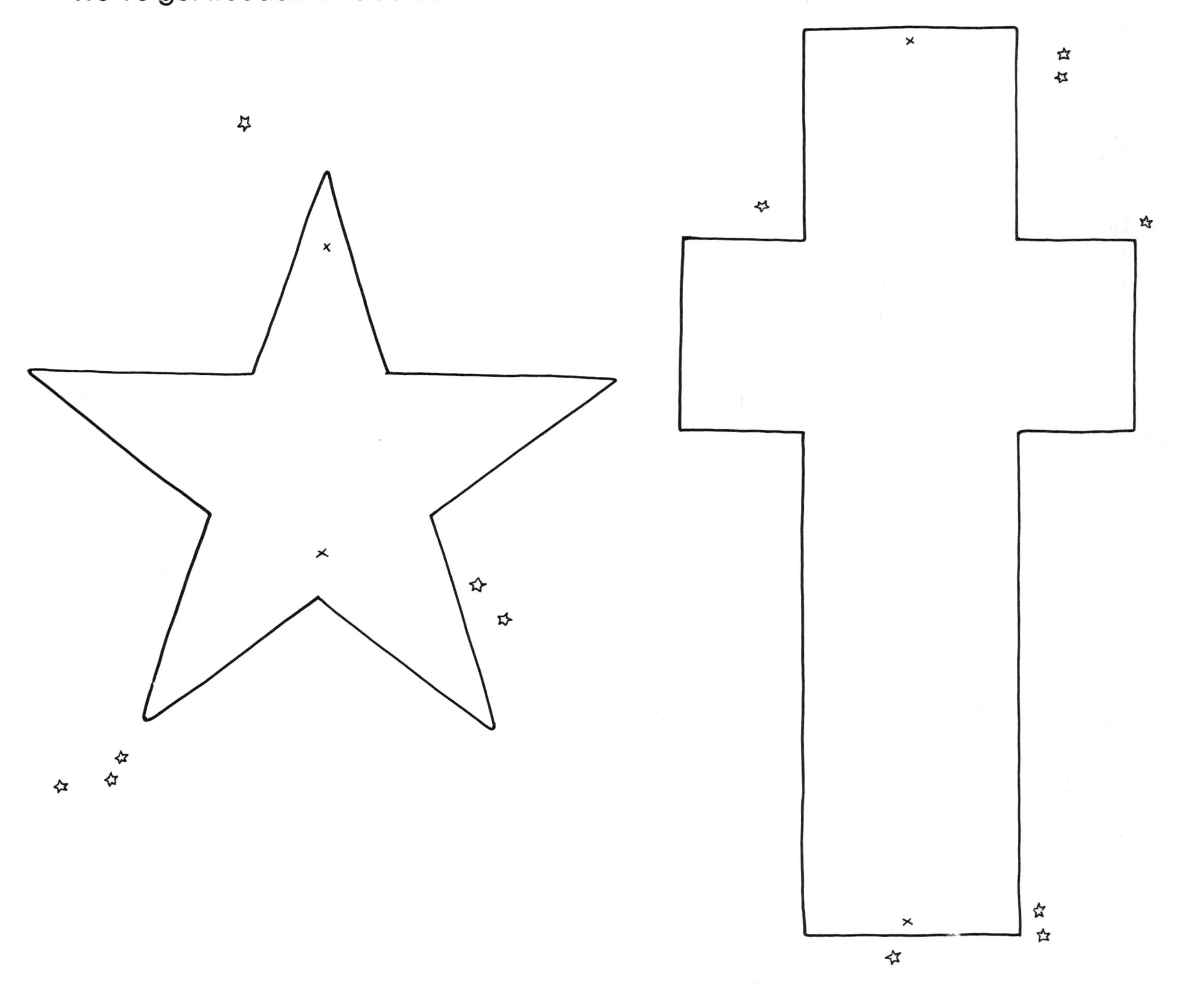

God's Knowledge

Timeless Truth

Nothing puzzles God.
(May be used at the beginning of the school year)

Bible Verse

"I am the LORD, the God of all mankind. Is anything too hard for me?"
Jeremiah 32:27

Bible Activity–Brain Drains!

Before Class

Gather these materials:
A string
A ring

During Class

Start with a game of "Ring on a String." Have everyone except the person who is "It" sit in a circle. The person who is "It" should be in another room or blindfolded during this setup. Put a ring on a long string which will stretch into a circle big enough for everyone to hold onto. The ring is hidden under someone's hand and passed along as secretly as possible. When "It" is in the circle, he must try to guess who has the ring. If, after a specified length of time, no correct guess has been made, choose a new "It" and let the former "It" sit in the circle.

Discussion

Was it hard to be in the circle?

Let's read Jeremiah 32:27. Does God ever get stumped or confused?

Did you know that God promises to give us wisdom if we ask Him?

Can God help you with school questions?

Digging Deeper

What is your most confusing subject at school? Does God know the answers to the questions you have?

What Bible characters asked God for help in confusing situations?

Personal Plan

Make a list of some things that puzzle you. Thank God that He knows all the answers. Copy Jeremiah 32:27 and read it over and over this week.

Needs

Timeless Truth

God wants me to actively come to Him for my needs.

Bible Verse

". . . Ask and it will be given to you; seek and you will find; knock and the door will be opened to you. For everyone who asks receives; he who seeks finds; and to him who knocks, the door will be opened." Luke 11:9-10

Bible Activity–Hide and Seek

Before Class

Hide little treasures such as stickers, erasers, candy, pencils, etc., around the room.

During Class

Spend a few minutes having the children tell knock-knock jokes. Tell some yourself. Knock on something each time for effect. Then have the children search around the room for the hidden treasures.

Discussion

You may want to let the children act out the following situations.

If you were lost in a busy store and needed help finding your parents, what would you do?

When you are hungry after school, what do you say to your mom?

If you were selling Girl Scout cookies and you needed to get your neighbor to answer the door, what would you do?

To find the treasures hidden in this room, what did you have to do?

Would just sitting and waiting work in any of these situations?

Let's read Luke 11:9-10. What does God's Word say about our actions?

Who wants us to be actively in touch with Him for everything?

Digging Deeper

What important thing did Nicodemus do in John 3:1-21? Was Jesus happy to spend time with him? What important thing did Zacchaeus do?

Personal Plan

Do you always remember to ask God about important things in your life? Talk to God and tell Him about every need you can think of. Copy Luke 11:9-10 and read it over and over this week.

Prayer

Timeless Truth

Because I'm His child, God hears me whenever I call.

Bible Verse

". . . God has heard your prayer . . . ."
Acts 10:31

Bible Activity–Don't Telephone . . . Tell God!

Before Class

Clean two food cans and remove the labels. (Make sure there are no sharp edges.) Cut a 20' piece of string. Punch a hole in the center of the end of each can. Push the end of the string through one can, and tie a large knot at the end of the string inside the can. Do the same with the second can.

During Class

Let students communicate across the room by talking into and listening through the cans. Let them try communicating on either side of a closed door also.

Discussion

Was it easy to hear each other?

Did your voices sound muffled?

Aren't you glad for real telephones?

Do we need a phone to talk to or to hear God?

How can we hear God?

Does God ever put us on hold?

Does God ever have an answering machine on?

Let's read Acts 10:31.

Digging Deeper

Who in the Bible is known for praying? Can you say the Lord's Prayer?

Personal Plan

Look in the Gospels and see how many times you read about Jesus praying. When do you pray? Make a list of things you want to talk to Jesus about; then talk to Him about them. Copy Acts 10:31 and read it over and over this week.

Light and Dark

Timeless Truth

People without Jesus in their lives live in darkness.

Bible Verse

"I will turn the darkness into light before them and make the rough places smooth. These are the things I will do; I will not forsake them." Isaiah 42:16b

A.

Bible Activity–The Gospel Glower

Before Class

Gather these materials:
Brown paper lunch bag for each child
Crayons or markers
Large rubber band or piece of yarn
Flashlight

During Class

Talk with the children to find out how they feel about light and dark, fear and bravery, clear pathways and confusing directions. Then read Isaiah 42:16.

Discussion

Who wants to make the way confusing for us?

Who wants us to be afraid in the dark?

Who wants us to worry about our future?

Who wants us to worry about where we'll go when we die?

Who wants us to live without fear?

Who wants us to look forward to heaven?

Let me show you a way to remember who can be more powerful in your life.

Demonstrate for the class how to put together the Gospel Glower as follows:

1. Draw a "reversible" face on a paper bag (figure A). "This sad, worried face makes me think of how the devil wants us to be."
2. Put the flashlight in the bag and secure the bag around it with a rubber band or string.

3. Hold the bag upside down to show the happy face (figure B). "This happy face makes me think of the plan Jesus has for our lives. And look what happens when we turn on the light. Those who know Jesus live in the light! Let's all make bags to take home today to remind us and others about the light of Jesus."

Give the children time to decorate their bags to take home and use with their own flashlights.

Musical Moment

Sing "This Little Light of Mine."

Digging Deeper

When do we first read about Satan in the Bible? What happened when the man and woman listened to him?

How did Satan try to tempt Jesus? Did Jesus give in to him?

Personal Plan

Do you know someone who does not have the light of Jesus? Show that person your "Gospel Glower" this week, and explain what Jesus did on the cross for everyone. Copy Isaiah 42:16b and read it over and over this week.

God's Protection

Timeless Truth

God is my safe hiding place.

Bible Verse

"You are my hiding place; you will protect me from trouble and surround me with songs of deliverance."

Psalm 32:7

Bible Activity–Hide and Seek and Peek

Before Class

Gather these materials:

Matching margarine tubs (or small milk cartons with the tops cut off)

Beans

During Class

Divide children into groups of two or more. Give each group three containers and a bean.

Show them how to hide the bean under one container; then quickly move the containers around to make those watching forget where the bean is.

Let every child have a turn at hiding the bean.

Discussion

How many of you tricked the others?

How many of you kept track of where the bean was?

Let's read Psalm 32:7. Who promises to hide us?

Can Satan find us to stir up our lives if God is hiding us?

Can God ever be tricked?

How does this verse make you feel?

Musical Moment

Sing these words to the tune of "Jingle Bells."

I am safe from all harm.
I am safe today.
God protects and guides in love;
He holds me all the way.

Digging Deeper

From whom did David have to hide? How did God protect him?

Personal Plan

Make a list of some people or things that scare you. Read the list to God as you pray. Thank Him for His promise of protection. Copy Psalm 32:7 and read it over and over this week.

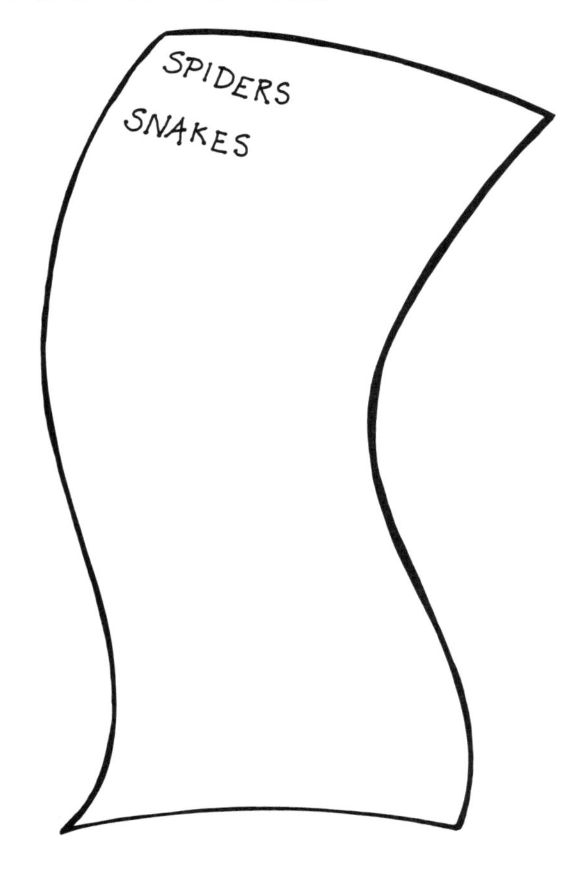

Speaking for God

Timeless Truth

I can trust God to help me know what to say.

Bible Verse

". . . Who gave man his mouth? Who makes him deaf or mute? Who gives him sight or makes him blind? Is it not I, the LORD? Now go; I will help you speak and will teach you what to say." Exodus 4:11-12

Bible Activity–Mighty Mouths

Before Class

Gather these materials:
Three paper plates per child
Stapler or hot glue gun
Markers or crayons

During Class

Hand out the paper plates to each child. Show how to staple the edges together (or hot glue them yourself for speed). Have the children draw and color features and tongues to make faces from the plates.

Let the children play with their completed face puppets for a few minutes.

Discussion

What have your puppets been talking about?

Who told them what to say?

Could they have talked without you?

Do you always choose your words carefully?

Who can help us say right things?

How do we learn to say the right things?

Musical Moment

Sing these words to the tune of "The Farmer in the Dell."

I sometimes feel I can't
Remember what to say.
But God can help me speak;
He's ready right away.

I sometimes feel I can't
Tell others of His love.
But God can help me speak;
He'll send help from above.

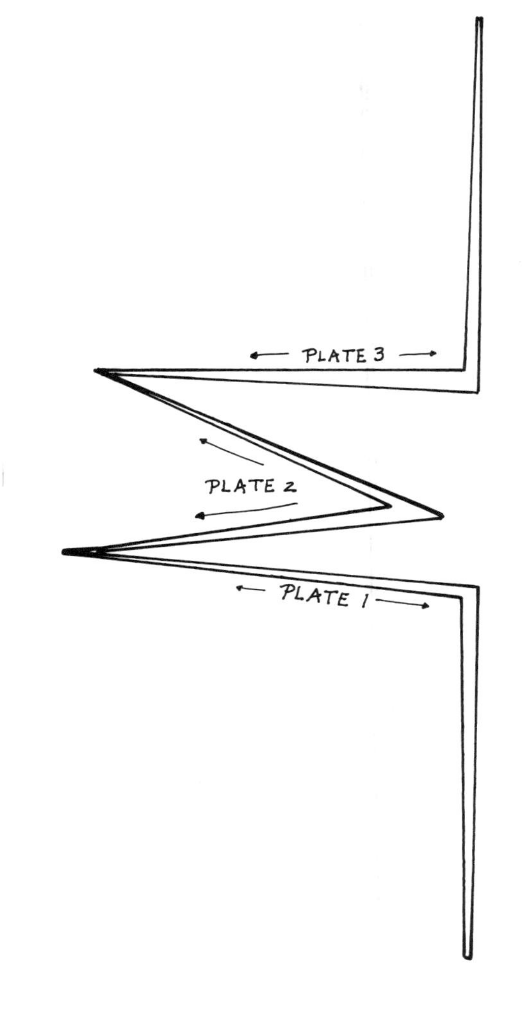

Digging Deeper

What man in the Old Testament wanted his brother to speak for him?

Name someone you know who definitely lets God speak through him.

Personal Plan

When have you been too afraid to speak? Have you been afraid to tell others about the Lord? Copy Exodus 4:11-12 and read it over and over this week.

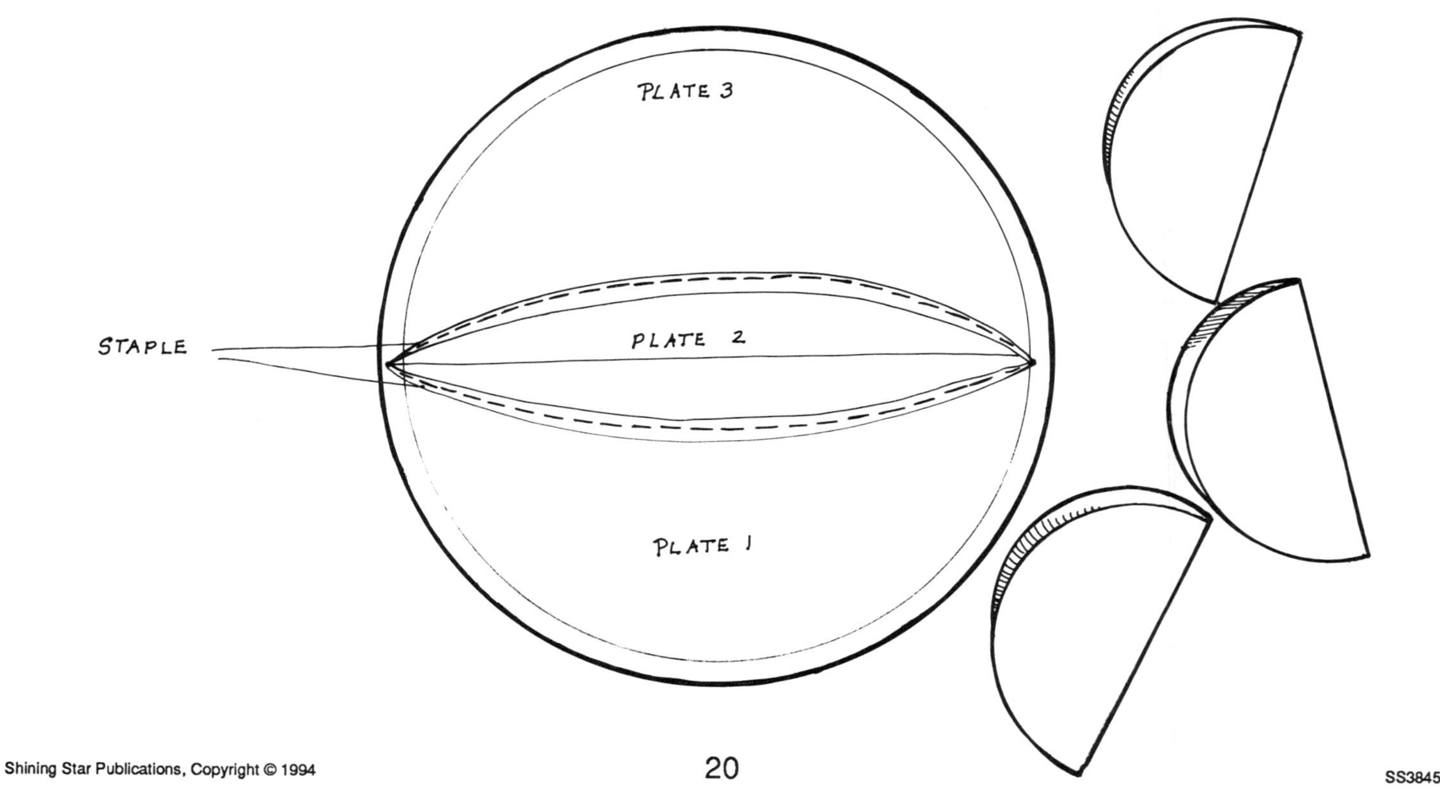

Thankfulness

Godly Goal

I want to remember to thank those who do things with me and for me.
(Veterans Day or Memorial Day)

Bible Verse

"I thank my God every time I remember you. In all my prayers for all of you, I always pray with joy because of your partnership in the gospel from the first day until now." Philippians 1:3-5

Bible Activity–Notes for the Notables

Before Class

Gather these materials:
Aluminum foil
4" circle to trace
Scissors
Glue
Pattern on page 22
Crayons or markers

During Class

Have the children list some people who help them or do things with them. Make a class list on a chart or a chalkboard.

Have the children color a thank-you note for each person they want to thank, gluing on aluminum foil for the "mirror."

Fold the notes and add addresses, or have the children plan to deliver the notes in person.

Digging Deeper

Read Psalm 100. What was the writer of the Psalm thankful for?

What New Testament writer often said "thanks" early in his letters?

Personal Plan

Who else can you thank this week? Make a list of ten people you will say "thank you" to this week.

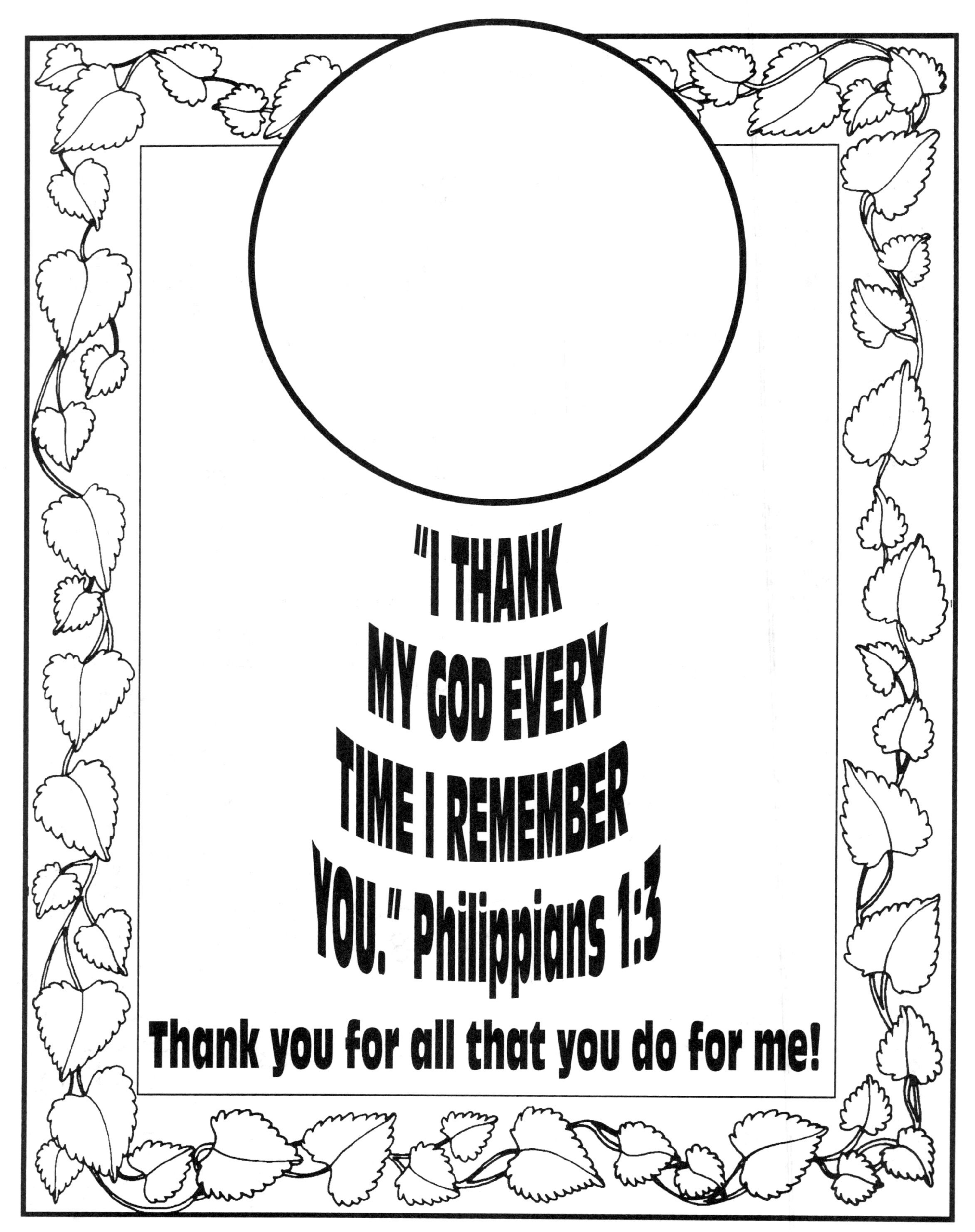
"I THANK
MY GOD EVERY
TIME I REMEMBER
YOU." Philippians 1:3
Thank you for all that you do for me!

The Armor of God

Timeless Truth
God is my strength and protection.

Bible Verse
". . . Be strong in the Lord and in his mighty power. Put on the full armor of God so that you can take your stand against the devil's schemes."

Ephesians 6:10-11

Bible Activity–God's Armor

Before Class
Gather these materials:
Light cardboard
Aluminum foil
Patterns on page 24
Scissors
Bible verse on the chalkboard
Yarn (12" long)
Glue or tape
Pencil
Markers

During Class

Discussion
What are some things that scare you?

Have you ever been afraid in the dark?

Did you know that the Bible talks about armor that we can wear to help us not be afraid? (Paraphrase Ephesians 6:10-18 or read it from the Bible.)

What part of God's armor sounds the best to you?

How do we put on this armor of God? (By asking Jesus to be our Savior, filling our minds with His words from the Bible, obeying His commands, and asking for His help.)

Art for the Heart

Have the children cut out the patterns below, trace them on light cardboard, and cut them out. Wrap pieces of aluminum foil around the sword and shield. Secure them with glue or tape.

Use a pencil to copy the Bible verse, Ephesians 6:10-11, on the shield. Then go over the words with a marker.

Tape a piece of yarn to the handle of the sword and the top of the shield so they can be hung over a doorknob as a reminder of God's armor.

Digging Deeper

Name as many Bible characters as you can who were probably afraid and put their trust in God for protection.

Personal Plan

What thoughts or feelings of fear will you turn over to God this week? Copy Ephesians 6:10-11 and read it over and over this week.

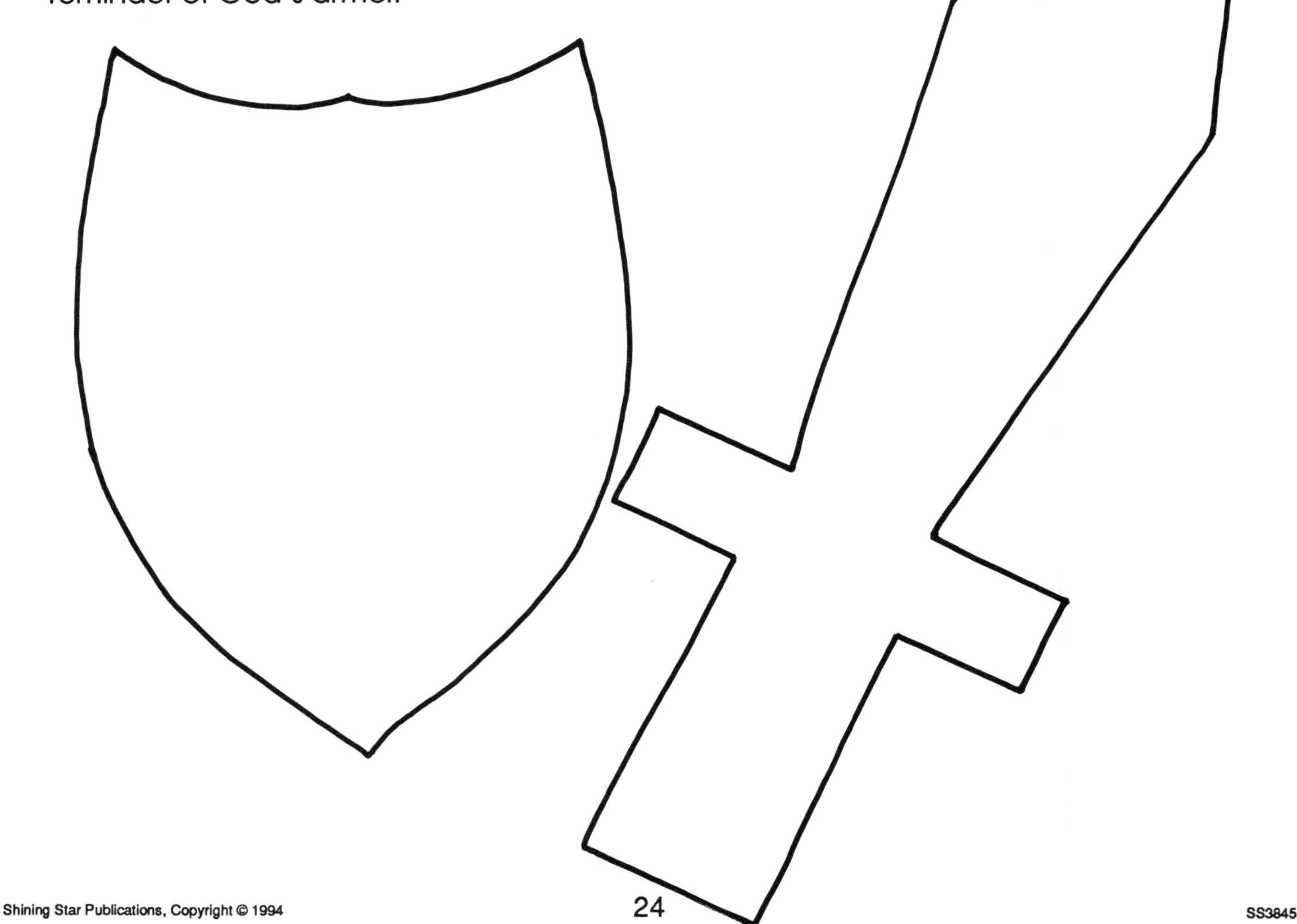

Forgiveness of Sin

Timeless Truth

Because of Jesus, no sin is too bad for God to forgive.

Bible Verse

"'Come now, let us reason together,' says the LORD. 'Though your sins are like scarlet, they shall be as white as snow; though they are red as crimson, they shall be like wool.'" Isaiah 1:18

Bible Activity–White as Snow

Before Class

Gather these materials:
Three clear quart jars (mayonnaise size)
3" x 7" strips of red cotton cloth
Bleach
Dish soap or detergent
Pitcher of water
Rubber gloves
Paper towels
Cookie sheet (to use as a work base)

Dip a piece of red cloth in bleach to make sure the color is affected.

During Class

Pretend you are doing a commercial for soap and bleach. Pour some bleach and a little bit of water into a jar. Pour some soap and water into another jar. Pour only water in a third jar.

Dip red cotton fabric in each jar.

Discussion

Which product would you buy for making this red cloth white?

Did the soap or water change the color of the cloth?

Let's read Isaiah 1:18 together. What does God say He will do with our sins?

Scarlet means red. Red is a color that is very noticeable. It sticks out. God is saying that even the most obvious sin can be completely erased by Him. How?

Let's read 1 John 1:9. Jesus came so that we could talk freely to God and confess our sins. What does He promise to do for us?

Musical Moment

Sing these words to the tune of "I'm a Little Teapot."

Jesus will forgive my saddest sin.
He'll gladly clean me up within.
I must say I'm sorry when I pray.
My sin's forgiven; it's chased away.

Jesus will forgive my saddest sin.
He'll change my frowning to a grin.
I believe He died for all mankind.
He is the best friend you can find.

Digging Deeper

What sad thing happened to Peter when Jesus was being tried before He died? How did Jesus respond to Peter's sin?

Name as many Bible characters as you can who failed Jesus. How many of them did He forgive?

Personal Plan

What do you need to talk to God about? Have you ever been afraid to tell Him about bad things you've done? Does He know about them already? Spend time confessing those sins to God. Copy Isaiah 1:18 and read it over and over this week.

Sin

Timeless Truth

My sin cannot be hidden from God.

Bible Verse

"And you may be sure that your sin will find you out." Numbers 32:23b

Bible Activity–The Nose Knows!

Before Class

Gather these materials:
Onion
Cinnamon sticks
Bottle of vanilla
Pine tree sprig
Orange
Coffee grounds
Containers with lids
Blindfold for each child

Cut the orange and the onion in half. Put each of the items in a tightly sealed container, such as a margarine tub or zip-top bag.

During Class

Keep the items out of sight and unopened as you tell the children that you want them to be nose detectives. Blindfold each child; then bring in the opened smelly items. Have the children walk around the room in a line trying to find the item that does not smell good. They must not use their hands.

Discussion

Which items smelled the best? Which one smelled the worst?

Was it easy to find the onion? Did you need your eyes or hands to tell it was an onion?

How do you think sin compares with an onion?

Is an onion easy to keep hidden? Is it easy to keep sin hidden from your parents? From God?

Let's read Numbers 32:23b. What does God's Word say about sin?

Let's read 2 Corinthians 2:15. What can we be if we are following Jesus' example?

Musical Moment

Sing these words to the tune of "Row, Row, Row Your Boat."

No, no, no you can't
Hide a secret sin.
God can see each thing you do
And hear your thoughts within.

Yes, yes, yes you can
Live a life that's right.
Read your Bible, pray each day,
Serve Jesus day and night.

Digging Deeper

Read about Ananias and Sapphira in Acts 5:1-10. What does their story teach you about trying to hide sins from God?

What brother in Genesis killed his brother and tried to hide from God?

Personal Plan

Confess your sins to God as soon as you realize you've done wrong this week. Copy Numbers 32:23b and read it over and over this week.

"Salt" for Jesus

Timeless Truth

When I speak and act in a way that pleases Jesus, I am salt, "seasoning" those around me for the best.

Bible Verse

"Let your conversation be always full of grace, seasoned with salt, so that you may know how to answer everyone."
Colossians 4:6

Bible Activity–Salt to the Rescue!

Before Class

Gather these materials:
6" string or sewing thread
Two or three ice cubes
A glass of water
Salt
Chalkboard and chalk or posterboard and markers

During Class

After you try this experiment on your own, gather the materials on a table for the class to see.

1. As you float the ice cube in the glass, talk to the children. People who don't have Jesus as their best friend are like ice cubes floating round and round in a glass of water.
2. Hang one end of the string over the edge of the glass.

   Jesus reaches out to those who don't know Him. He shows them the beauty of His creation around them daily. He sends His love through you, through your words and actions.
3. Place the other end of the string on the ice cube and sprinkle it with a little salt. As Christians, we are to be salt. To be salty means to live in obedience to Jesus' words so that others see Him in our words and actions.

   Let's leave this salty ice cube for a few minutes and think of ways we can be salty.

Digging Deeper

Take five or ten minutes to help the class make two lists: one of friends and family who need Jesus as their best friend and one of things that they can do and say to show Jesus' love. Help the children think of ways to be salty and draw others to Jesus. Give them a chance to copy some of the ideas from the board, if there is time.

Personal Plan

Come back to the experiment to show the children that the salty string has stuck to the ice cube.

Saltiness has drawn the string and cube together, just like you can draw others to Jesus!

Jesus Is Christmas

Godly Goal

I want to think more about Jesus at Christmas time.

Bible Verse

"But Mary treasured up all these things and pondered them in her heart."

Luke 2:19

Bible Activity–Thaumatrope

Before Class

Gather these materials:

A copy of the pattern on page 31 for each child
A pencil for each child
Tape
Scissors
Glitter
Glue
Markers or crayons

During Class

Read Luke 2:19 to the class. Talk about some things that may cause us to forget about Jesus' birth at Christmas time.

Hand out the pattern for the children to color and decorate.

Place a pencil on the back side of one of the pictures and tape it securely. Give each one a pencil also. Place a pencil on the back side of one of the pictures and tape it securely. Fold on the broken line and tape the ends together.

Musical Moment

Sing these words to the tune of "Are You Sleeping?"

What a treasure, what a treasure
Jesus is, Jesus is!
He is the great reason
To celebrate the season.
He came down,
Left His crown.

What a treasure, what a treasure
Jesus is, Jesus is!
He is like a present
That the Lord of heav'n sent.
He came down,
Left His crown.

Digging Deeper

Who brought treasures to the young Jesus?

Who waited in the temple to see Jesus dedicated?

Personal Plan

Take your pencil and thaumatrope to school. Use it as a reminder that Jesus is the reason for Christmas. Copy Luke 2:19 and read it over and over this week.

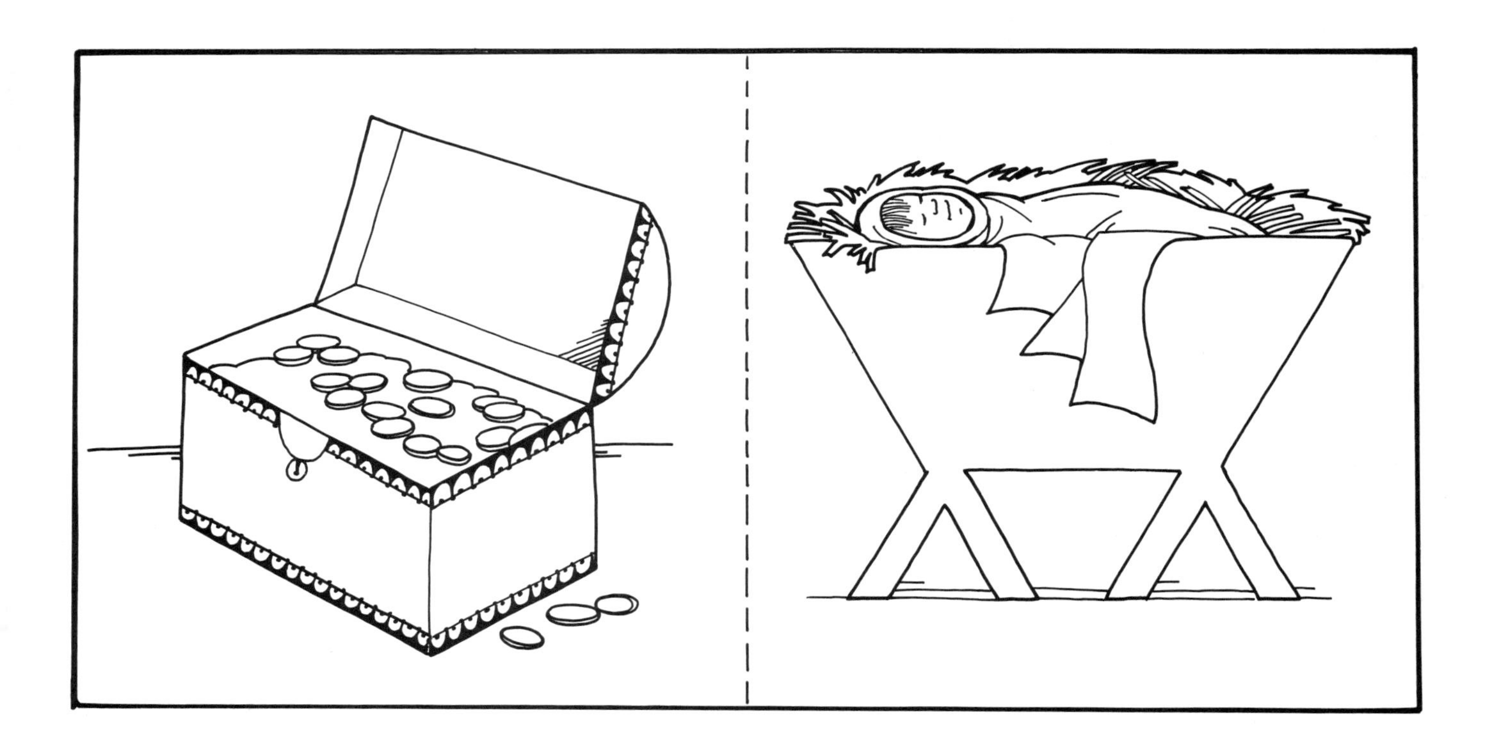

God Knows Me

Timeless Truth

People see my appearance; God sees my heart.

Bible Verse

"The LORD does not look at the things man looks at. Man looks at the outward appearance, but the LORD looks at the heart." 1 Samuel 16:7b

Bible Activity–Envelope Detectives

Before Class

Gather these materials:
One envelope per child
Keys
Coins
Combs
Charge cards
Paper clips
Safety pins
Crayons or pencils

Put one of the small flat items in each envelope and seal it.

During Class

Tell the children you want them to be envelope detectives. They may look only at an envelope, without touching it, and guess what is in it. Then they may hold the envelope on two corners and shake it and guess what is inside. Then they may rub a crayon or pencil over the envelope and guess what is in it.

Finally, open the envelope to see if their guesses were right.

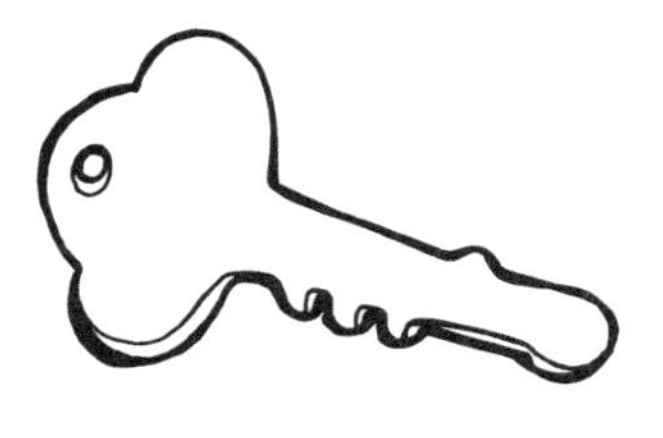

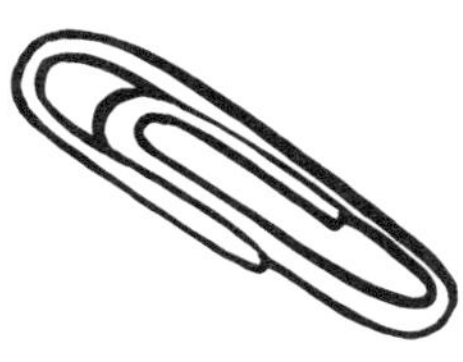

Discussion

Was it difficult to tell what was in the envelope using the first two methods? When did you finally know what was inside? Who knew for sure what was in the envelopes from the beginning? How did you know?

How are we like these envelopes? How does God know what we are like inside?

Psalm 139 tells us that He knows what we are physically like inside. Let's read 1 Samuel 16:7 to see what else God knows about us.

Digging Deeper

Can we know what people's hearts are like? What does James 1:5 say about asking for wisdom?

Personal Plan

How does it make you feel to know that God knows your heart? Does that make it easier when people don't understand you? Copy 1 Samuel 16:7b and read it over and over this week.

Worry

Godly Goal

I want to live a long life, understanding the power of God.

Bible Verse

"But seek first his kingdom and his righteousness, and all these things will be given to you as well. Therefore, do not worry about tomorrow . . . ."

Matthew 6:33-34

Bible Activity–Paper Plate Pals

Before Class

Prepare puppets, using the patterns on pages 95-96; copy the script; and make a stage for presenting the skit.

During Class

Patty: (in a worried voice) I wonder if it's going to rain tomorrow. I'm so worried. Oh, what will I do if it rains? I sure hope it doesn't rain tomorrow. I've worked so hard planning the Girl Scout picnic. What will I do? Oh, I sure hope it doesn't rain. Have you heard the forecast?

Pete: Patty, what are you so worried about? If the Lord wants it to rain tomorrow, then it will all work out. He'll provide another day that will work for your picnic. Don't worry.

Patty: You're right, Pete. I wonder how I'm going to do on my math test on Monday. It's going to be hard. I just hope I don't blow it. I'm really worried. I really am. I'm no good at numbers. They are so confusing! Oh, dear.

Pete: Patty, what are you so worried about? Just study; then ask the Lord to help you do your best. That's all you can do. Don't worry; the Lord cares about your test. He wants you to do your best, doesn't He?

Patty: You're right, Pete. I sure hope I don't get the flu. It's going around you know. All those germs flying around, in the air. I think I just heard someone sneeze. Oh, I hope I don't get sick. I hate the flu. Did I hear another sneeze?

Pete: Patty, you sure worry a lot. If you get the flu, God will take care of you. Besides, don't you know that God controls everything that comes into your life? He promises that He won't let anything come your way that you cannot handle with His help. Do you believe that, Patty?

Patty: Oh, Pete, I guess I am a worrier. I forget how big God is! He is all powerful. Why should I worry? I feel better already. I feel like the sun has come out from behind the clouds. God is so big, isn't He?

Pete: That-a-girl, Patty!

Discussion

Let's read Proverbs 10:27 and Matthew 6:33-34. According to these verses, what adds length and health to our lives?

What does it mean to fear the Lord? It's believing that God is in control, isn't it?

How do you feel about your life when you're worrying?

How do you feel about your life when you are believing in God's great care for us?

God blesses our lives when we trust in Him!

Musical Moment

Sing these words to the tune of "Zacchaeus."

God's taking care of me every day;
He watches day and night.
He won't let anything come my way
That for me isn't right.
He'll give me strength for all that's tough;
He'll help me when it's hard.

(spoken)
And He'll say, "My child, don't you worry!
I'm in charge of all your days.
I'm in charge of all your days."

Digging Deeper

Think of some Old Testament people who lived a long time. Were their lives full of worry? What does Matthew 6:25-34 say about worry?

Personal Plan

What do you worry about? Write your worry on a piece of paper and throw it in the trash to show that you'll trust God and throw away that worry. Copy Matthew 6:33-34 and read it over and over this week.

Enemies

Godly Goal

I want to be kind to my enemies and let God take care of their reward or punishment.

Bible Verse

"If your enemy is hungry, give him food to eat; if he is thirsty, give him water to drink. In doing this, you will heap burning coals on his head, and the LORD will reward you." Proverbs 25:21-22

Bible Activity–Finger Friends Fight

Before Class

Prepare puppets, using the patterns on pages 95-96; copy the script; and make a stage for presenting a skit.

During Class

Fred: (Holding a piece of wadded-up paper) Hey, who ruined my letter to Grandma? I've worked on this for days!

Fern: I did. It was so sloppy!

Fred: Fern, you're mean! I could just . . . just . . . just . . .

Fern: You could just what? You can't hurt me.

Fred: (quietly) I just thought of something. I learned in Sunday school that I am supposed to be kind to those who hurt me. This is hard but, Fern, I forgive you!

Fern: You what?

Fred: I forgive you, Fern. I'm just going to start over. I guess I could do it more neatly.

Fern: Fred, are you feeling OK?

Fred: Yes, I am. Would you like some cookies? My mom just baked them.

Fern: Fred, I think I need to go to church with you this Sunday. I think I'd like to learn to be nice like you. Yes, I'd love a cookie!

Discussion

How would you feel if someone destroyed something of yours?

Would it be hard to be kind to the person who did it?

Let's read Proverbs 25:21-22. What does God command us to do to our enemies?

What will God do if we obey?

Where can we get the strength we need to love our enemies?

Digging Deeper

Why was it amazing that Jesus talked to the Samaritan woman at the well?

Why was it amazing that the Good Samaritan helped the wounded man?

Personal Plan

Think of some people who have mistreated you. What can you do for them? Who will take care of your reward and theirs? Copy Proverbs 25:21-22 and read it over and over this week.

Giving Cheerfully

Godly Goal
I want to be an enthusiastic giver.

Bible Verse
". . . Whoever sows sparingly will also reap sparingly, and whoever sows generously will also reap generously . . . for God loves a cheerful giver." 2 Corinthians 9:6-7

Bible Activity–Finger Friends Fun

Before Class
Prepare puppets, using the patterns on pages 95-96; copy the script; and make a stage for presenting the skit.

Gather these materials:
Construction paper
Glue
Cotton swabs for applying glue
Margarine tubs for glue
Seeds of various colors

During Class
Fred: Hey, Fern, what are you looking at on the ground?

Fern: Ah, Fred, I've been coming here every day for a week to look at this spot.

Fred: What's so neat about this spot? It just looks like some dirt to me. There's not even any grass.

Fern: Last week I planted a pumpkin seed and I'm waiting for it to grow.

Fred: Did you water it?

Fern: Yes!

Fred: Did you cover it with soil?

Fern: Yes!

Fred: What could be the problem?

Fern: Wellllllll . . . .

Fred: Well, what?

Fern: I did see Fanny's pet squirrel digging over here later that same afternoon.

Fred: Aha! But he probably took only one seed. You surely planted more, didn't you?

Fern: Well, no, I only planted one and threw the rest away.

Fred: Fern, don't you remember our Bible verse?

Fern: You mean the one about fixing holes in socks?

Fred: Don't be silly! The verse was, "Whoever sows sparingly will also reap sparingly, and whoever sows generously will also reap generously." That applies to giving an offering, giving our service, and planting seeds! Not sewing up holes in old socks!

Fern: Oh, dear, I was so looking forward to pumpkin pie!

Discussion

Do you ever give just a little of yourself? Is that the way God wants us to serve Him?

What happens when we obey God with enthusiasm?

Giving just a little is like planting only one seed. Sometimes it works, but sometimes it doesn't. It's always better to give all you can.

Art Activity

Have the children draw pictures of flowers. Use glue and various colored seeds to outline or fill in the flowers.

Digging Deeper

How do you feel when someone does something with you in an unenthusiastic way? Who are some Bible characters who gave of themselves enthusiastically?

Personal Plan

What are some things you've been doing for the Lord halfheartedly? Will you try to start doing them with more enthusiasm? Copy 2 Corinthians 9:6-7 and read it over and over this week.

Helping Others

Timeless Truth

God wants me to help those in need.

Bible Verse

"Suppose a brother or sister is without clothes and daily food. If one of you says to him, 'Go, I wish you well; keep warm and well fed,' but does nothing about his physical needs, what good is it? In the same way, faith by itself, if it is not accompanied by action, is dead."

James 2:15-17

Bible Activity–Ministry Mural

(This project may be worked on for short amounts of time over a few weeks.)

Before Class

Gather these materials:
Fabric scraps or wallpaper samples
Magazines and clothing catalogs
Scissors
Glue or staples
Markers or crayons

Prepare a large bulletin board with a light blue background or place a large sheet of paper of light blue on the wall. Glue on cotton batting to look like snow across the bottom.

During Class

Read James 2:15-17 to the class.

How would you feel if you were outside on a cold day without warm clothes? What if you had to sleep outside where it was cold? Have you ever been so hungry that your stomach wouldn't stop growling?

Let's make a mural that reminds us about how we are to help people in need.

Give each child a magazine and a catalog. Have him cut out two people: one to represent himself and one to represent a needy person. Provide fabric scraps or wallpaper samples for making clothes. The child may also draw a house and food or cut them from the magazine. Glue the completed figures and house to the mural.

Musical Moment

Sing these words to the tune of "Away in a Manger."

Some people are hungry.
Some people need clothes.
Some people are homeless.
So what if it snows?

The answer is easy;
God makes it quite clear.
Those people need our help
So they will not fear.

Digging Deeper

What woman in the New Testament was known for her good deeds for others? Read Acts 9:36-39 to find out. Who did the disciples find out needed help in Acts 6:1?

Personal Plan

Ask your parents for ideas about ways you can help needy people. Make a list of the things you and your family can do.

Encouraging Others

Godly Goal

I want to be a missionary of encouragement.
(St. Patrick's Day)

Bible Verse

". . . Paul sent for the disciples and, after encouraging them, said good-by and set out for Macedonia. He traveled through that area, speaking many words of encouragement to the people, and finally arrived in Greece." Acts 20:1-2

Bible Activity–"I Care Cards"

Before Class

Gather these materials:
A copy of the "I Care Card" on this page for each child
Scissors
Markers or pens
Envelopes

During Class

Saint Patrick was a missionary and an encourager to the people of Ireland as Paul was in Acts 20:1-2. Let's read those verses.

Today we're going to make "I Care Cards" to give to the people we are around. We'll cut them out and then put an encouraging Bible verse or truth on the back of each one.

Have the children copy Bible verses such as Jeremiah 29:11; 1 Samuel 16:7; or 2 Thessalonians 3:3 on the backs of their cards.

Digging Deeper

What Bible characters besides Paul can you name who encouraged others? Who encourages you?

Personal Plan

Make a list of some people you think need to be encouraged. Pray for a missionary you know who is encouraging people far away.

What Jesus Gave Up

Timeless Truth

Jesus left the richness of heaven to be a poor man on earth for us.

Bible Verse

"For you know the grace of our Lord Jesus Christ, that though he was rich, yet for your sakes he became poor, so that you through his poverty might become rich." 2 Corinthians 8:9

Bible Activity–Crown to a Creche

Before Class

Trace the pattern on page 44 for yourself and practice changing the crown to a creche (manger scene). Trace another pattern to use in class.

(Optional: Make a pattern for each child to try.)

During Class

As you slowly cut out the crown, talk to the children.

What do you think heaven is like? Are there mansions there? What kind of people do you think of when you think of mansions? Do rich people wear crowns?

Do you think Jesus wore a crown in heaven? (Complete your cutting at this question.)

Where was Jesus born? Was it like a mansion?

Do you think it smelled good?

Who lived there before Jesus came?

Was it very different than heaven? (Complete folding the crown into a stable shape at this point.) Let's read 2 Corinthians 8:9 together.

Did Jesus give up a lot to come to earth and be born in a stable? Most importantly, how did Jesus' life end? What was His last crown like?

Digging Deeper

Did Paul follow Jesus' example of giving up good things? Did Moses live in a palace?

Personal Plan

How can you follow Jesus' example in your life? Make a list of right things that are not easy to do. Are you willing to do them? Copy 2 Corinthians 8:9 and read it over and over this week.

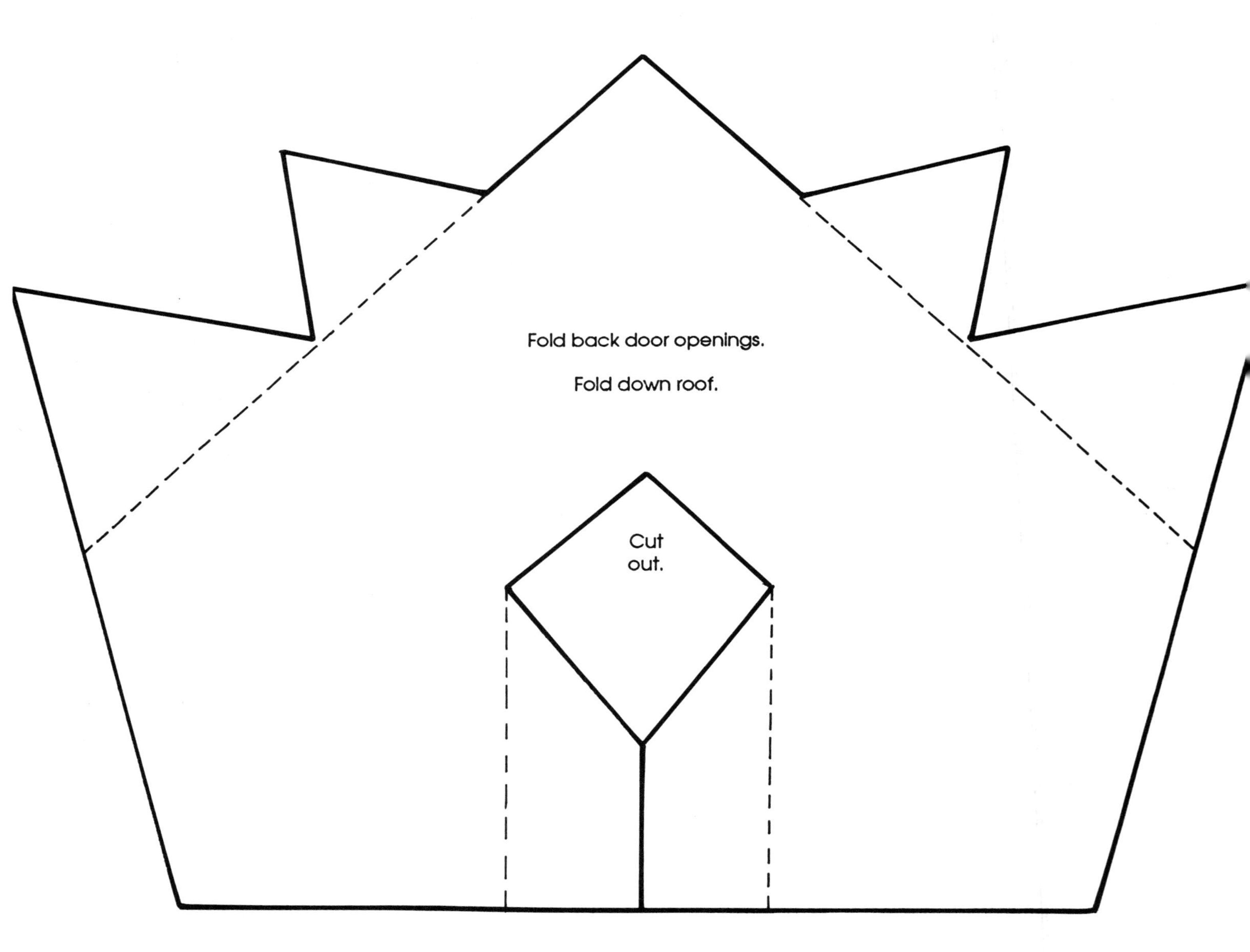

God's Truth in My Heart

Timeless Truth

God writes His truth in my heart.

Bible Verse

"You show that you are a letter from Christ, the result of our ministry, written not with ink but with the Spirit of the living God, not on tablets of stone but on tablets of human hearts."

2 Corinthians 3:3

Bible Activity–Carbon Copy Art for the Heart

Before Class

Gather these materials:
Carbon paper
Pencils
White paper
Crayons
Paper clips

During Class

Give each child some carbon paper, white paper, and paper clips. Show how to make a picture by drawing on the back of the carbon paper.

Have each child take a plain piece of white paper and color it completely, pressing hard with the crayons, leaving no uncolored surface.

Use this piece of colored paper as carbon paper with another piece of white paper clipped underneath.

Discussion

Would carbon paper work without someone writing on it?

Carbon paper is somewhat like the Holy Spirit. He is ready to make copies of truth on our hearts if someone will just get the pencil moving! When we read the Bible He prints God's truth on our hearts.

When we listen to someone teach the stories of the Bible, the Holy Spirit prints the truth on our hearts.

Continue the art activity by having the children copy 2 Corinthians 3:3 on a sheet of white paper using carbon paper or their rainbow paper.

Musical Moment

Sing these words to the tune of "Silent Night."

Write on my heart
Every part
Of Your truth
That I need.

God, I want You to teach me what's good,
So I'll know how to do what I should.
Thanks for sending Your Spirit
To write Your word on my heart!

Digging Deeper

What is your favorite Bible verse that the Holy Spirit has written on your heart? What can you do to make God's truths stick in your mind longer?

Personal Plan

Hang your carbon copy verse where you will see it a lot this week, and remember how God wants to write more and more of His truth on your heart.

Helping the Weak

Timeless Truth

God will reward me for taking care of the weak.

Bible Verse

"Blessed is he who has regard for the weak; the LORD delivers him in times of trouble. The LORD will protect him and preserve his life; he will bless him in the land and not surrender him to the desire of his foes." Psalm 41:1-2

Bible Activity–Real Life or Drama?

Before Class

Ask someone confined to a wheelchair or crutches to visit your class. If you are unable to find someone who is permanently or temporarily handicapped, ask someone to pretend. Ask the visitor to talk with the children about how it feels to be handicapped. Have a brief discussion with the children before the visitor arrives. Make some slings out of fabric scraps ahead of time for them to try.

During Class

Start class by telling the story of David's kindness to Mephibosheth in 2 Samuel 9.

Discussion

How do you think it would feel to be handicapped and not have the use of your arms or legs?

Would you like to try it? Hand out slings to be used on arms or tied around feet. Let the children practice doing things without using a hand or foot.

Put the slings away before the visitor arrives. Allow the children to ask the visitor as many questions as possible in the time available.

Digging Deeper

How did Jesus respond to people with physical weaknesses?

Personal Plan

What can you do this week to help someone who is weaker than you? Copy Psalm 41:1-2 and read it over and over this week.

Love

Godly Goal

I want my love to be unselfish.

Bible Verse

"Love is patient, love is kind. It does not envy, it does not boast, it is not proud. It is not rude, it is not self-seeking, it is not easily angered, it keeps no record of wrongs. Love does not delight in evil but rejoices with the truth. It always protects, always trusts, always hopes, always perseveres. Love never fails.

1 Corinthians 13:4-8a

Bible Activity–Skit with Paper Plate Pals

Before Class

Prepare puppets, using the patterns on pages 95-96; copy the script; and make a stage for preparing the skit.

(Optional: Write 1 Corinthians 13:4-8a on the chalkboard.)

During Class

Patty: Pete, I saw you take a cookie today after Mom said not to. I'm going to tell on you when she gets home from the store. In fact, I'm going to wait right here by the door!

Pete: You make me so mad! You're always tattling on me! Are you glad when I get in trouble?

Patty: Sure! Of course, I hardly ever get in trouble myself. I'm so good.

Pete: Well, believe it or not, I wish I could do better at obeying Mom.

Patty: Ha! That'll be the day!

Pete: I think I'll start today! Even if you do tell on me, I'm going to tell Mom that I'm sorry. Tomorrow is a new start. Hey, here comes Mom now!

Discussion

Who was supposedly the naughty person?

Let's read 1 Corinthians 13:4-8a.

Who was closer to having the right kind of love, Pete or Patty?

What are some loving things Patty could have said instead of giving Pete a hard time?

Musical Moment

Sing these words to the tune of "I've Been Working on the Railroad."

We can learn to love each other
All the livelong day.
Reading over First Corinthians thirteen
Shows us the way!

We should never boast or tattle.
We should think of ways
To protect our friends and family
And end our selfish days!

Digging Deeper

Who always loves us with the kind of love in 1 Corinthians 13? Who are some people you know who show unselfish love?

Make up a new puppet script with a friend based on 1 Corinthians 13:4-8. Act it out with puppets.

Read 1 Corinthians 13:4-8. Put your name in place of the word *love*. Are there some things in your life that you need to work on to be more loving?

Personal Plan

What things can you change in your life this week to become less selfish and be more loving instead? Copy the part of 1 Corinthians 13:4-8a that you want to work on and read it over and over this week.

Faith

Godly Goal

I want to have faith in God to please Him.

Bible Verse

"And without faith it is impossible to please God, because anyone who comes to him must believe that he exists and that he rewards those who earnestly seek him." Hebrews 11:6

Bible Activity–Giving God the Best Gift!

Before Class

Wrap two sets of gifts for your class. One set should be paper crosses with the word *FAITH* printed on each of them. The other set should be two small candy canes for each child.

Display the gifts in two separate piles for the children to see as they enter. Also have a small Christmas tree nearby.

During Class

Sit down near the gifts with the children and ask some questions.

Who likes gifts? What do you think might be in this package? (Shake one of the candy cane packages.) Let's each open a package. (Hand a candy cane package to each child.)

These candy canes remind us of Jesus, God's gift to us. See the "J" shape? (Hold up a candy cane.)

What gift can we give God to please Him? Let's read Hebrews 11:6 to find out.

What is faith? Faith is believing that God loves us; wants to take care of every part of our lives; and has sent His Son, Jesus, to provide our salvation. It means trusting that what God says in His Word is true.

Who would like to open another gift? (Hand out the FAITH packages.) Who should receive this gift?

Shall we put this gift under the tree for God? Let's also each hang one candy cane on the tree to remind us of Jesus. Take the other candy cane home to remind you all week of the great gift of Jesus.

Musical Moment

Sing these words to the tune of "B-I-N-G-O."

God gave to us the greatest gift.
He gave us His dear Son.
J-E-S-U-S,
J-E-S-U-S,
J-E-S-U-S,
He gave us His dear Son.

God asks that we give faith to Him
And trust Him with our lives.
F-A-I-T-H,
F-A-I-T-H,
F-A-I-T-H,
And trust Him with our lives.

Digging Deeper

Talk about how the wise men and the shepherds showed that they had faith in God.

Name some Bible characters who had faith, and tell how their lives showed their faith in God.

Personal Plan

What can you do this week to reach your Godly Goal? Copy Hebrews 11:6 and read it over and over this week.

Heaven

Timeless Truth

As a Christian, I can look forward to my home in heaven with Jesus.

Bible Verse

"In my Father's house are many rooms; if it were not so, I would have told you. I am going there to prepare a place for you."
John 14:2

Bible Activity–Buildings and Bridges

Before Class

Gather these materials:
Drinking straws
Scissors
Paper clips

During Class

Demonstrate to the children how to construct buildings and bridges with paper clips and straws. The easiest method is to attach two paper clips together, then stick them into the ends of straws. (See the sketch on page 53.) Straws may be cut for a variety of shapes. Allow the children to work on their projects for about ten minutes.

Discussion

Which is easier–constructing buildings or bridges? What are the strongest buildings and bridges made of?

Let's read John 14:2 to find out about a building that has already been finished in heaven.

Do you think the buildings in heaven will ever wear out? Why?

Is it possible to build a bridge to heaven? Who is our bridge to heaven?

Musical Moment

Sing to the tune of the "Alphabet Song."

Jesus has prepared a place,
And I'll have a special space
Just for me
As His child
I will be there quite a while.
Jesus has prepared a place
And I'll have a special space.

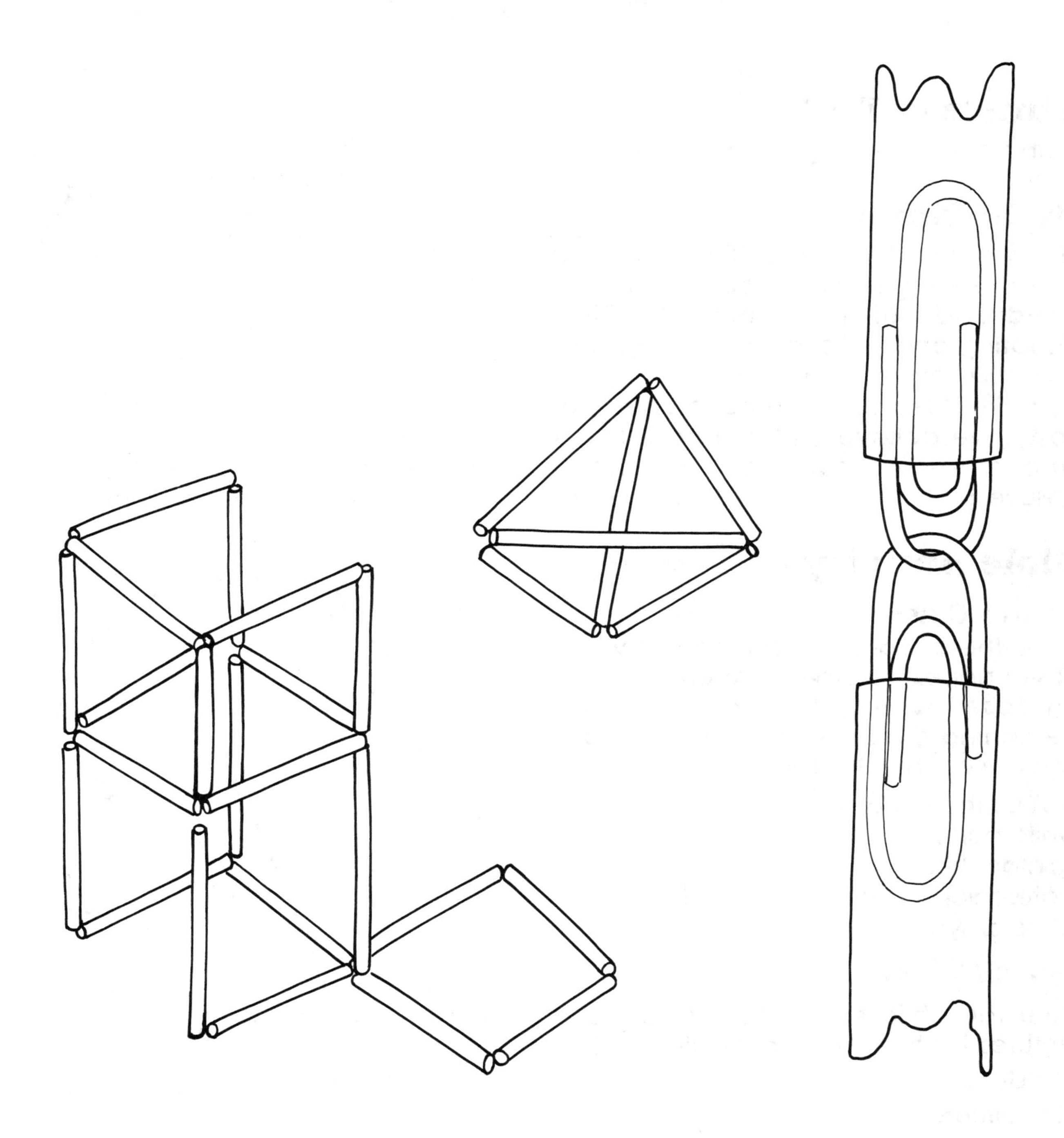

Digging Deeper

Name as many people as you can who are already in their heavenly rooms. How can we make sure we have a room in heaven?

Personal Plan

Why do you think heaven will be nice? What are some things you will be happy to leave behind? Copy John 14:2 and read it over and over this week.

What Is Faith?

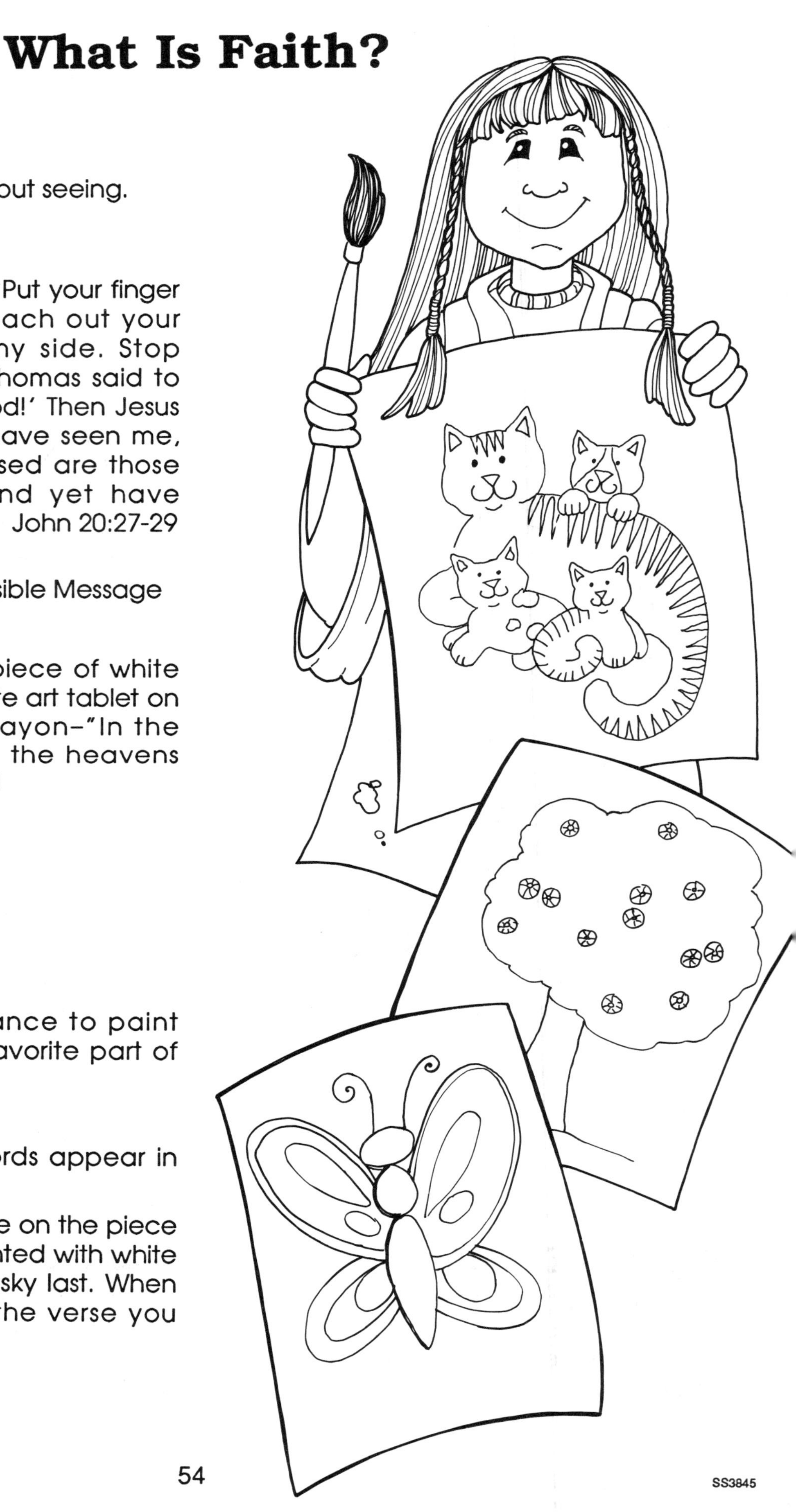

Timeless Truth

Faith means believing without seeing.

Bible Verse

"Then he said to Thomas, 'Put your finger here; see my hands. Reach out your hand and put it into my side. Stop doubting and believe.' Thomas said to him, 'My Lord and my God!' Then Jesus told him, 'Because you have seen me, you have believed; blessed are those who have not seen and yet have believed.'" John 20:27-29

Bible Activity–Invisible Message

Before Class

Write these words on a piece of white poster paper (or large white art tablet on an easel) with white crayon–"In the beginning God created the heavens and the earth." Genesis 1:1

Gather these materials:
White paper
Paintbrushes
Watercolor paints
White crayons

During Class

Give the children a chance to paint pictures illustrating their favorite part of spring.

Discussion

Would you like to see words appear in the sky when I paint?

Paint a simple nature scene on the piece of paper on which you printed with white crayon, painting the blue sky last. When you paint the sky blue, the verse you printed will appear.

Who believed I could make words appear? What is it called when you believe something without seeing it first?

Let's read John 20:27-29 to find out about Thomas' faith and what Jesus said to him. Did Thomas have faith at first?

Is God pleased when we have faith without having to be shown?

Digging Deeper

How did Noah show his faith? How did Daniel show his faith in the lions' den? How did Mary the mother of Jesus show her faith?

Personal Plan

Do you ever doubt God? Do you want to have more faith like Noah or Daniel? Copy John 20:29 and read it over and over this week.

Trusting God

Timeless Truth

When I trust in God, He will help me overflow with hope.

Bible Verse

"May the God of hope fill you with all joy and peace as you trust in him, so that you may overflow with hope by the power of the Holy Spirit." Romans 15:13

Bible Activity–Bubbling Over!

Before Class

Gather these materials:
An 8 oz. clear juice glass
Vinegar
Baking soda
Powdered sugar
Measuring cup
Teaspoon
Cookie sheet
Paper towels

During Class

Today we are going to try an experiment with a few simple kitchen items.
Have the children help you with these steps:

1. Place the juice glass on the cookie sheet.
2. Pour ⅓ c. vinegar into the juice glass.
3. Add one heaping teaspoon of baking soda.
4. Watch out!

Repeat steps one and two. For step three, add powdered sugar and observe the different reaction in the mixture.

Discussion

Which ingredient when mixed with the vinegar caused it to bubble over?

Baking powder and powdered sugar look similar, but they don't react in a similar way with vinegar, do they?

People sometimes get God and good things mixed up. They think doing good things will give joy, peace, and hope that overflow. But only trusting in God can give those things.

Musical Moment

Sing these words to the tune of "If You're Happy and You Know It."

If you're trusting in the Lord each day,
  Hurray! (Clap! Clap!)
If you're trusting in the Lord each day,
  Hurray! (Clap! Clap!)
If you're trusting, You'll be busting
Out with joy and peace and hope.
If you're trusting in the Lord each day,
  Hurray! (Clap! Clap!)

Digging Deeper

Who in the book of Acts were so filled with joy that even in jail they sang?

Do you think we can have joy and hope even when we are sick? Why?

Personal Plan

How can you show others your joy, peace, and hope this week? If you're lacking any of those qualities, spend time praying and asking God to help you trust Him more. Copy Romans 15:13 and read it over and over this week.

Giving Brings Blessings

Timeless Truth

Giving in any way brings blessing back to me.
(May Day)

Bible Verse

"Give, and it will be given to you. A good measure, pressed down, shaken together and running over, will be poured into your lap. For with the measure you use, it will be measured to you." Luke 6:38

Bible Activity–May Basket

Before Class

Gather these materials:
Pattern on page 59 for each child
Markers
Glue
Scissors
Construction paper or wallpaper samples
Confetti popcorn

Recipe for confetti popcorn

1. Pop corn in a convenient manner to yield 4 to 6 cups.
2. Place the popcorn on a cookie sheet sprayed with non-stick cooking spray.
3. In a 2-cup glass measuring cup combine ¼ c. granulated sugar, one drop of food coloring, and ¼ c. water.
4. Microwave on high for 7 to 8 minutes or until the sugar starts to turn dark. (Watch carefully, so burning does not occur.)
5. Drizzle the syrup over the popcorn.
6. Repeat steps 3, 4, and 5, but use a different color of food coloring.
7. When the popcorn is cool break it into small pieces.

During Class

Demonstrate how to make a May Day cone as follows:

1. Glue the cutout pattern on a piece of construction paper and cut around it.
2. Put a thin layer of glue along the side of the cone and press the two sides together.
3. Cut a paper strip and glue it on the cone for a handle.
4. Fill the cone basket with confetti popcorn.

Help the children make these May Day cones.

Discussion

Read Luke 6:38.

Who likes to receive special surprises? How do you feel toward people who give you special surprises? According to Luke 6:38, what happens when we give anything to others?

To whom can you give your May Day cone?

What is something else we can give to others?

Digging Deeper

What did the wise men give to Jesus? How do you think they felt when they saw Him? How did God reward the wise men?

Personal Plan

What are some ways you can give of yourself to people this week? Whom can you thank who gives of himself or herself to you? Copy Luke 6:38 and read it over and over this week.

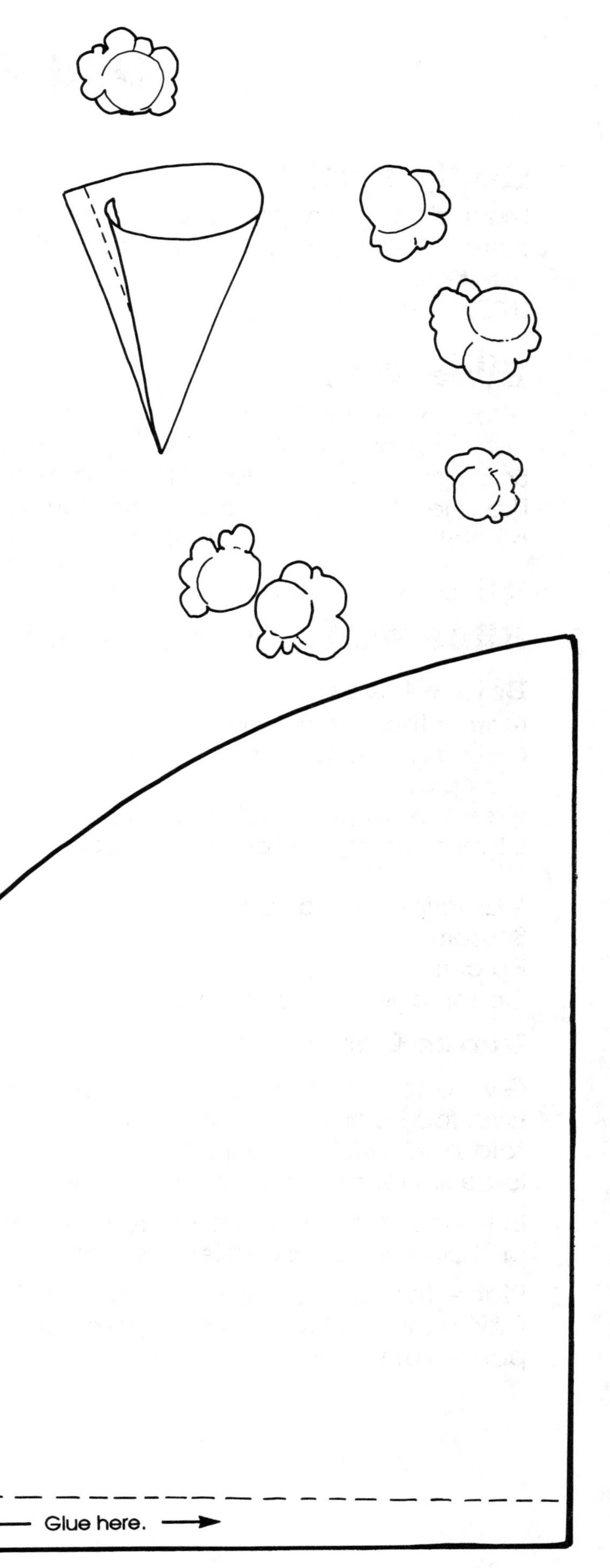

God Provides

Godly Goal

I should not worry because God will take care of me just like He does all of creation.
(May Day)

Bible Verse

"Consider how the lilies grow. They do not labor or spin. Yet I tell you, not even Solomon in all his splendor was dressed like one of these . . . how much more will he clothe you, O you of little faith!"
Luke 12:27-28

Bible Activity–Art for the Heart

Before Class

Gather these materials:
Colorful fabric scraps or wallpaper samples
Green felt or construction paper
Cloth covered wire cut in 8" pieces
Glue
Margarine tubs for glue
Scissors
Floral tape
Cotton balls or small pom-poms

During Class

Give each child five pieces of covered wire, fabric, and felt. Demonstrate how to fold and twist the wire to make three large flower-petal shapes and two leaves.

Bend the stems in a ninety-degree angle, and dip the petals and leaves in glue.

Place the glue-covered petals on the fabric and the leaves on the green felt or paper. Let the glue dry.

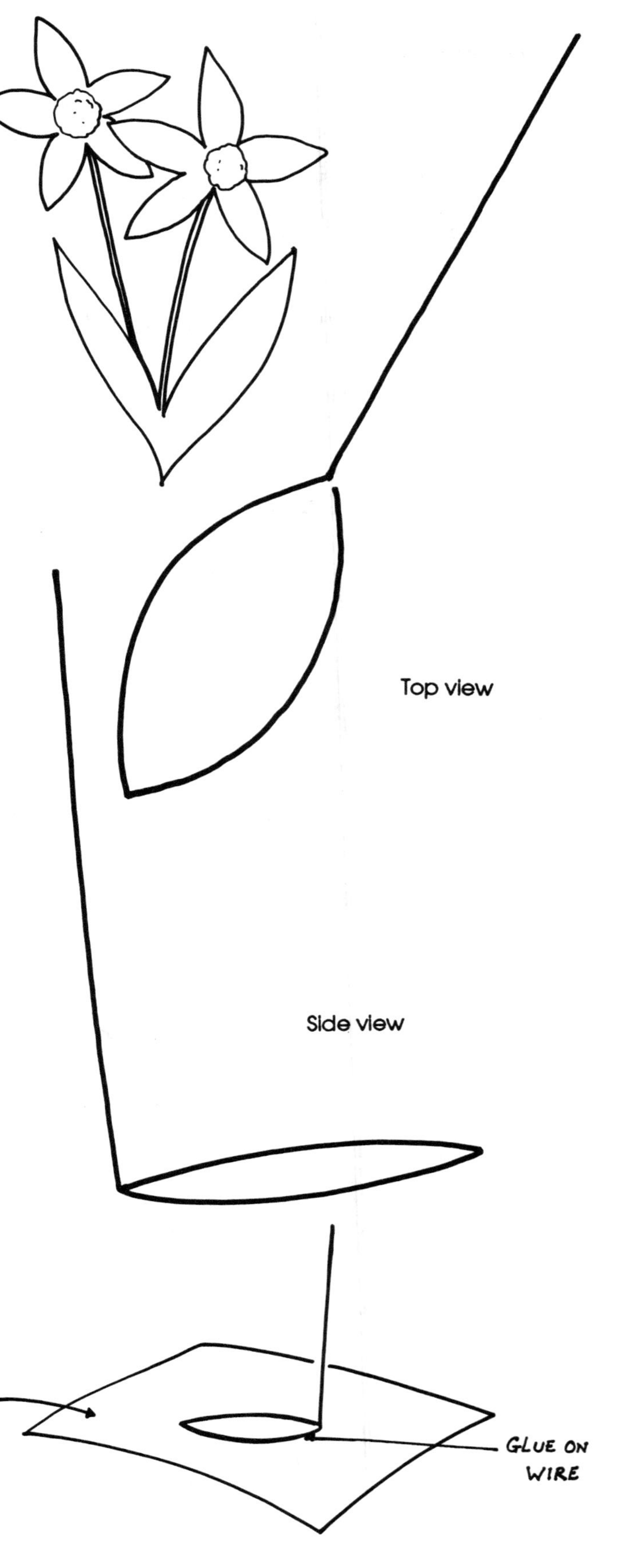

Discussion

What do you worry about? What you'll have to eat tomorrow? What you'll wear? Who will be your friend?

Let's read Luke 12:27-28. What does God's Word say about worrying? What should we look at to remind us that God will take care of us in all areas of our lives?

Musical Moment

Sing these words to the tune of "Did You Ever See a Lassie?"

Have you ever seen a flower, a flower, a
 flower?
Have you ever seen a flower
That needed to cry?
I think not.
I know so.
'Cause God's Word, it says so.
And just like all the flowers,
God cares for me too.

Let's complete our flowers and use them to remind us that God is able to take care of all our needs just as He cares for everything around us.

Do you know someone who needs these flowers for a reminder that God cares?

Show the children how to cut around the wire, tape the stems together, and glue the cotton ball in the center of the flower.

Digging Deeper

What does the Bible say about God and sparrows? Does God know what is going to happen to you tomorrow?

Personal Plan

Make a list of what God provides for you in your life. Use this list as you pray to thank Him. Copy Luke 12:27-28 and read it over and over this week.

Running God's Race

Timeless Truth

Life is like a race in which I'm representing God's team.

Bible Verse

"I have fought the good fight, I have finished the race, I have kept the faith."
2 Timothy 4:7

Bible Activity–Flopping Fish Race

Before Class

Put a masking tape line on the floor at one end of the room to be the finish line.

Gather these materials:
Newspapers
Scissors
Pencils
Ruler
Magazine

During Class

1. Have each child cut a 14" fish from a piece of newspaper.
2. Have everyone line up at the end of the room opposite the finish line.
3. At the word "go," each child blows his fish along by flapping a magazine.
4. The first one over the finish line wins.

Discussion

Try this crazy race a few times; then talk with the children about other races they have been in. Talk about team spirit. Then read 2 Timothy 4:7 and talk about being on God's team.

Digging Deeper

What are your favorite sports teams? Does it help the teams to have fans cheering for them? Who cheers for us on God's team? Who cheered for Jesus on Palm Sunday? Do we always have people cheering for us?

Personal Plan

What friends are on God's team with you? What are some things that you think are hard to do on God's team? Copy 2 Timothy 4:7 and read it over and over this week.

The Way to God

Timeless Truth

Jesus is the only way to God.

Bible Verse

"Jesus answered, 'I am the way and the truth and the life. No one comes to the Father except through me.'" John 14:6

Bible Activity–Ladder Lesson

Before Class

Practice cutting out a ladder and a cross using the patterns on page 64.

During Class

With every "yes" answer to the following questions, cut out a rung of the paper ladder.

Are you kind to animals?

Have you cleaned your room lately?

Have you said something nice to someone this week?

Have you prayed this week?

Have you read a Bible verse this week?

Have you helped someone this week?

When the questions have all been answered by the children, your ladder should be finished. Some people think doing good things like those you've done will be like a ladder to get them into heaven. Is that true? No. Let's read John 14:6. You can't climb to heaven on a ladder of good works!

Paraphrase Ephesians 2:8-9. Talk about the story of the tower of Babel in Genesis 11:1-9.

Discussion

Cut out a cross shape as you ask these questions:

Who died on the cross for the forgiveness of our sins?

Who is the one way to God and heaven?

Digging Deeper

What did Jesus tell Nicodemus? What did Jesus tell the repentant criminal on the cross?

Personal Plan

Have you tried to be good to earn your way to heaven? Have you asked Jesus to take charge of your life? Read John 3:16, Ephesians 2:8-9, and John 14:6 this week.

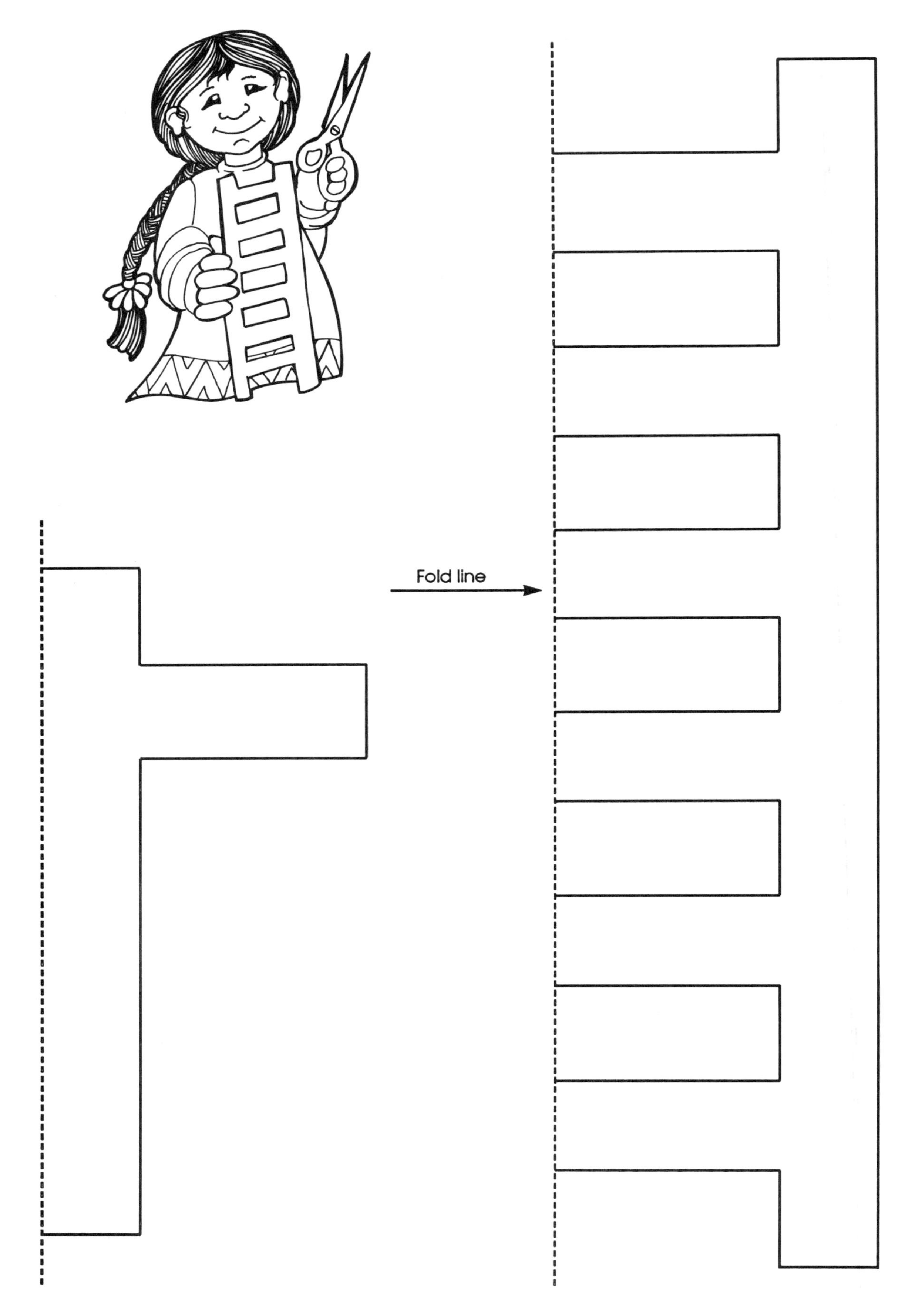
Fold line

Honoring Parents

Timeless Truth

God tells me to obey and honor my parents.
(Mother's Day or Father's Day)

Bible Verse

"Children obey your parents in the Lord, for this is right." Ephesians 6:1

Bible Activity–Presents for Your Parents

Before Class

Wrap a medium-sized prize in a box in newspaper. Continue to wrap it in extra sheets of paper. Between each layer of wrapping put a small present such as candy, balloons, or stickers, or a piece of paper with a penalty written on it. Use penalties such as "Stand on one leg and count to twenty-five" or "Bark ten times like a dog."

During Class

1. Choose a child to be in charge of a tape player, to stop and start the music.
2. Have the children sit in a circle and begin passing the package.
3. When the music stops, the child holding the package takes off one layer of wrapping and receives a prize or a penalty. If it's a penalty, the child must do what it says.
4. Then the music starts again, and the game continues.
5. The child who unwraps the last layer gets to keep the prize.

Discussion

Do you like getting prizes?

Do you like getting penalties?

How would you like to receive a prize every morning when you got up?

Would you rather have someone greet you with a penalty?

Did you know that you give your mom and dad a prize or a penalty every day?

When you wake up in the morning and start the day out obediently, you give them a prize! When you wake up with a grumpy, disobedient attitude, you give them a penalty! So what can you do to give prizes instead of penalties to your parents?

Digging Deeper

What kind of child was Jesus? Was He obedient to His earthly parents? Was He obedient to His heavenly Father?

Personal Plan

What do your parents ask you to do in the mornings? Make a list of responses that would be prizes for them. Copy Ephesians 6:1 and read it over and over this week.

Respect for Elders

Godly Goal

I should show respect for adults.
(Grandparent's Day)

Bible Verse

"Rise in the presence of the aged, show respect for the elderly and revere your God. I am the LORD." Leviticus 19:32

Bible Activity–Finger Friends

Figure It Out

Before Class

Prepare puppets, using the patterns on pages 95-96; copy the script; and make a stage for presenting the skit.

During Class

Fred: Hi, Fern. What do you have in your hand?

Fern: (A list should be attached to the puppet's hand.) I have made myself a "to do" list of all the things I want to do this year.

Fred: What's on your list?

Fern: I want to learn to sew some . . .

Fred: (interrupting) Oh, my grandma sews the neatest things. Last year she made me three outfits, a bedspread, and a tent!

Fern: Goodness, Fred, your grandma sounds amazing! Well, next on my list is planting a garden of . . .

Fred: (interrupting again) Oh, my great-aunt Fiona has the most beautiful flower garden in her backyard. She wins awards every year. I just love to go there and see the flowers and all the butterflies.

Fern: She sounds amazing! Next on my list is building a large dollhouse for my . . .

Fred: (interrupts again) Oh, have you ever met my Grandpa Frank? He is the most talented woodworker! He showed me how to use all the tools in his wood shop this summer.

Fern: (sounding a bit exasperated) Fred, I'm not going to tell you any other things on my list because you keep interrupting me. (thoughtfully) But, you have told me some neat things about some older people in your life. You're lucky! I guess I never realized what I could learn from older people. And Fred?

Fred: Yes, Fern.

Fern: I think you need to find someone older to teach you some manners!

Discussion

Talk with the children about all the special things elderly people have to offer. Then talk about how life is harder for elderly people (getting around, hearing, seeing, living alone).

Digging Deeper

Have an elderly person come in after the skit to answer questions from the children. List some people in the Bible who served God in a mighty way when they got older.

Personal Plan

Make a list of some elderly people you know. Write beside each name some special skills that person has. Make a plan for how you can learn from them. Copy Leviticus 19:32 and read it over and over this week.

Living a Godly Life

Godly Goal

I want to be pure and godly by living according to God's Word.

Bible Verse

"How can a young man keep his way pure? By living according to your word. I have hidden your word in my heart that I might not sin against you."

Psalm 119:9, 11

Bible Activity–Tied to the Truth

Before Class

Gather these materials:
Rolls of crepe paper
Rolls of curling ribbon

Cut the crepe paper and ribbon into many 12" strips and scatter them around the room before the children arrive.

Make a chain of ribbon strips, typing the ribbons securely. Keep it out of sight until later.

During Class

Divide the children into groups of three or four. Ask them to make chains from the strips they find around the room. Show them how to tie the pieces together securely with knots.

When the chains have all been connected, ask the children to have a tug-of-war with their chains. (The chains will break.)

Take out the chain of curling ribbon and show how much stronger it is.

Discussion

Do you know what these strips remind me of? The crepe paper reminds of things in my life that don't make my life better in a godly way because they tear apart so easily when stretched.

What are some of those things? (money, popularity, strength, etc.)

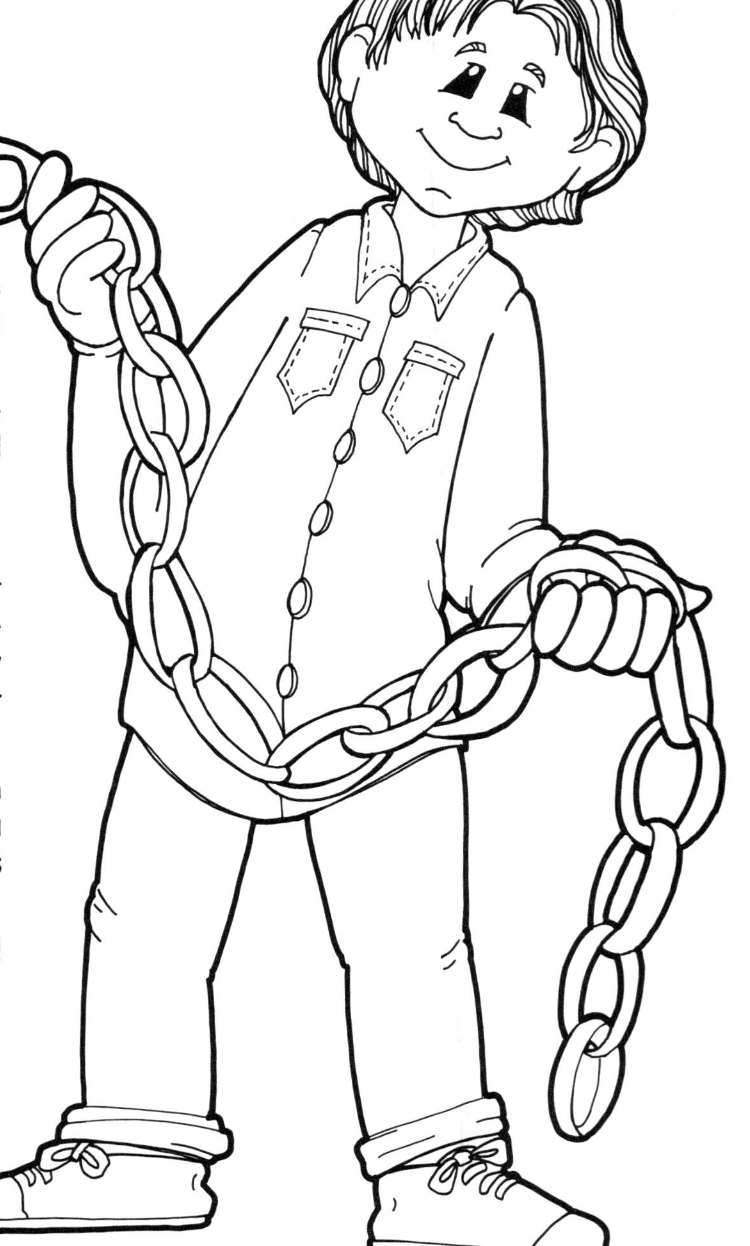

The ribbon reminds me of something that will always show me how my life can be more godly and not come apart easily. Do you know what that is? It is God's Word. God's Word helps me do what is right, such as being pure and not sinning.

Let's read Psalm 119:9 and 11 to find out how we can be godly.

Digging Deeper

How did Samson fill his life with ungodly things? What happened to him?

Personal Plan

Make a list of some Bible verses you have hidden in your heart (memorized). Make a list of verses you would like to memorize. Start this week. Copy Psalm 119:9, 11 and read it over and over this week.

Imitating Jesus

Godly Goal

I want to be like Jesus so others can see Him through me.

Bible Verse

"Follow my example, as I follow the example of Christ." 1 Corinthians 11:1

Bible Activity–A Sticking Impression

Before Class

Gather these materials:
Margarine tub
Liquid starch
White glue
Food coloring
Measuring cups
Comic books or comics from the newspaper
Baggies

During Class

Give each child ⅛ cup of liquid starch and ⅛ cup of white glue in a margarine tub. Have children "knead it" until it is well blended. It will be bouncy and will take impressions from comics. Let the children experiment for a few minutes; then give them baggies to put their "globs" in.

Discussion

Would you like to be a glob?

I wish I could pick up things the way the globs picked up the pictures.

Do you know what kind of pictures I wish people saw in my life? I would like them to see Jesus in me. How could people see Jesus in my life? How do we know what Jesus is like?

Let's read 1 Corinthians 11:1.

Digging Deeper

What people remind you of Jesus? What Bible character reminds you the most of Jesus?

Personal Plan

Ask God to make you more like Jesus this week. Look for verses about Jesus in the Gospels that tell you what you can imitate from His life.

Sharing the Way of Salvation

Timeless Truth

Jesus died for me and for the whole world.

Bible Verse

"For God so loved the world that he gave his one and only Son, that whoever believes in him shall not perish but have eternal life." John 3:16

Bible Activity–Color Cards

Before Class

Gather these materials:

Two or three copies of the card pattern (page 72) for each child

Red, white, black, gold, and green ribbon cut in 5" pieces

Medium-sized safety pins

Markers or crayons

Scissors

During Class

Recite John 3:16 with the children. Hand out the card patterns. Have the children make Color Cards to give to their friends.

Follow these steps.

1. Color the boxes by the Bible verses the appropriate colors.
2. Fold the card accordion style as illustrated.
3. Tie a ribbon of each color on the safety pin.
4. Attach the pin on the outside cover of the card as illustrated.

Have the children practice telling one another what the colors stand for.

Digging Deeper

Who were the first people in the New Testament to tell others about Jesus? Read Luke 2:20 to find out.

Do you think Jesus knew how big the world was when He spoke the words in Matthew 28:19-20?

Personal Plan

Who needs your Color Card and pin more than anyone else you know? Pray for that person. Pray for the missionaries who are sharing far away.

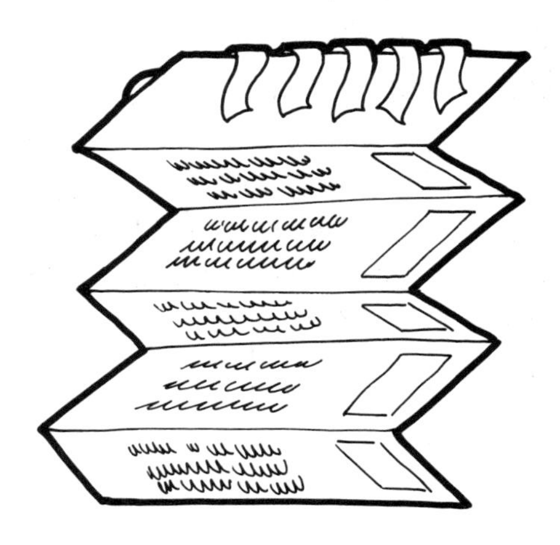

Fold

I do wrong things!
I need to be sorry
and realize I am
separated from God.

(Romans 3:23; John 8:21, 24)

Black for sin

Fold

Jesus' blood was shed
on the cross for my sins
so that I can be forgiven.

(John 3:16; Ephesians 2:8)

Red for blood

Fold

Jesus' death makes it
possible for me to be
as clean as snow inside!

(Isaiah 1:18)

White for clean

Fold

If I ask Jesus to be
my Savior, He promises
I'll be in heaven someday.

(John 14:2-3)

Gold for heaven

Fold

Now I need to pray and
read my Bible to grow
closer to Jesus, my Savior
and friend.

Green for growth

Christian Unity

Timeless Truth

Christians need to be united in their work for the Lord.

Bible Verse

". . . There should be no division in the body . . . you are the body of Christ, and each one of you is a part of it."

1 Corinthians 12:25, 27

Bible Activity–Slipping Clips!

Before Class

Cut a strip of paper 11" x 3" for each child and one for yourself. Have two paper clips for everyone also.

During Class

Demonstrate the amazing slipping clips as follows:

1. Curve your strip of paper as in the illustration.
2. Clip the paper clips to the paper as in the illustration.
3. Hold the ends of the paper and pull firmly but slowly.
4. The paper clips will fly off the paper and connect.

Let the children try the slipping clip trick for a while.

Discussion

Did you know that children of God are to be like these paper clips?

Paraphrase 1 Corinthians 12. How are we to be like paper clips?

Are we supposed to be divided from other Christians?

Can Christians disagree? Are we all exactly alike?

Let's be like these paper clips, working together with other Christians.

Digging Deeper

What Bible characters worked together? Did Joseph and his brothers work together? What caused the division in their family? How did that division affect Joseph?

Personal Plan

Make a list of your Christian friends. How are they different from you? What are some ways you can work together? Copy 1 Corinthians 12:25, 27 and read it over and over this week.

Listening

Godly Goal

I should be quick to listen and slow to speak to please God.

Bible Verse

". . . Everyone should be quick to listen, slow to speak and slow to become angry, for man's anger does not bring about the righteous life that God desires." James 1:19-20

Bible Activity–A Game of Gossip

During Class

Have the children sit in a line on the floor. Whisper a sentence in the ear of the first child and ask that it be whispered down the line one by one. The first time, have them whisper the sentence as quickly as possible down the line. The second time, ask them to whisper the message slowly.

Discussion

Did the message change by the end of the line? Why? Did it change more when you talked faster or slower? Did it come out more clearly when you went slowly?

Let's read James 1:19-20 in our Bibles. How does our game remind you of what this verse teaches? How can we change our everyday speech to please God?

Digging Deeper

How did Peter show that he needed to work on being slow to speak when he denied Jesus?

Did Adam and Eve listen quickly to God or Satan? How could things have been different for them?

Personal Plan

Make a list of the people to whom you need to be quick to listen. Copy James 1:19-20 and read it over and over this week.

God Made Me

Timeless Truth

God knows me perfectly because He made me.

Bible Verse

"O Lord, you have searched me and you know me. For you created my inmost being; you knit me together in my mother's womb. My frame was not hidden from you when I was made in the secret place." Psalm 139:1, 13, 15a

Bible Activity–Man-Made Microscope

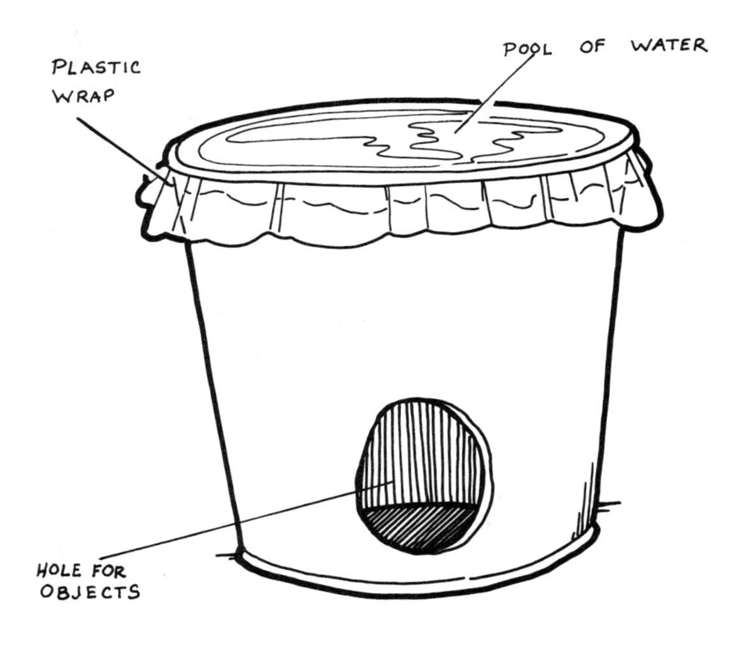

Before Class

Gather these materials:

A large plastic pail in which you have cut 2 or 3 large holes
Plastic wrap
String or a large rubber band
Water
Small interesting objects for magnification

During Class

1. Stretch the plastic wrap loosely across the top of the pail, and fasten it securely with a large rubber band or string.
2. Pour water on the plastic wrap.
3. Put objects you would like to magnify in the pail through the holes. Look at them through the water-covered plastic wrap.

Discussion

Can we find out all the details of these objects with our microscope?

Can scientists find out all the details of objects with their powerful microscopes?

Let's read Psalm 139:1, 13, and 15. How much does God know about us? How does that make you feel?

Digging Deeper

List the things God created in the six days of Creation. How did He make Adam and Eve different?

Personal Plan

Make a list of things to talk to God about. Be sure to tell Him thanks for the parts of your life that you especially like. Tell Him about the areas in which you need help. Thank Him that He knows everything about you. Read all of Psalm 139 this week.

Good Out of Bad

Timeless Truth

God takes what looks bad and makes it good in my life.

Bible Verse

"You intended to harm me, but God intended it for good to accomplish what is now being done." Genesis 50:20a

Bible Activity–Paper Plate Pals

Before Class

Prepare puppets, using the patterns on pages 95-96; copy the script; and make a stage for presenting the skit. Add a bush and a wooden box to the scene.

During Class

Patty: (crying) I just fell down and skinned my knee!

Paul: Patty, are you OK? How did it happen? Did you trip?

Patty: Yes, I tripped over a wooden box here near this bush. I didn't see it as I skipped by.

Paul: Did you say a wooden box?

Patty: Yes, a wooden box! I sure wish I had seen it. My knee hurts.

Paul: Patty, I have been hunting everywhere for this wooden box. I have all my savings from mowing lawns this summer in it. I guess I left it here after that last time I mowed our lawn! I have over $50 in it.

Patty: Fifty dollars! Wow, Paul, I can't believe it.

Paul: In fact, this is so wonderful, I'm going to treat you to some ice cream. Here comes the ice cream man right now.

Patty: My knee is feeling better already!

Tell the story of Joseph's life. End it by reading Genesis 50:20.

Discussion

Discuss what happened to Patty and how God is at work in all situations for good. Give everyone a bandage as a reminder of the story.

Musical Moment

Sing these words to the tune of "Kum Ba Yah." (Remind the children that *Kum Ba Yah* means "Come by here, Lord.")

Yesterday was hard,
Kum ba yah.
I fell in my yard,
Kum ba yah.
The new neighbor came,
Kum ba yah,
To help me,
Kum ba yah.

We had never met,
Kum ba yah.
He had no friends yet,
Kum ba yah.
Now we're going to be,
Kum ba yah,
Best buddies,
Kum ba yah.

Digging Deeper

What are some difficult situations you have experienced that turned out for your good and the good of others in the end?

What Bible characters went through hard situations and became stronger?

Personal Plan

Make a list of difficult things you have experienced. Beside each, write something good that came from it. Copy Genesis 50:20a and read it over and over this week.

No Complaints!

Godly Goal

I want to do things without complaining or arguing, so I can shine like a star.

Bible Verse

"Do everything without complaining or arguing, so that you may . . . shine like stars in the universe." Philippians 2:14-15

Bible Activity–Don't Whine, Shine!

Before Class

At least 48 hours before class make a star as follows:

1. Gather glitter, waxed paper, and glue.
2. Use the glue to make star shapes (they don't have to be perfect) on the waxed paper, and sprinkle them with glitter. Make sure the glue is completely covered.
3. After 48 hours, carefully peel the waxed paper from the back of the star, working in from each point.

Hang your finished stars in a window or from the ceiling.

Collect art materials for the children so they can make stars.

During Class

Demonstrate how to make stars. Allow the children to make two or three stars each.

Discussion

Do you think stars are special to see? Have you ever watched stars at night? Do you know any of their names?

What makes stars seem so bright? Is it the darkness?

Let's read Philippians 2:14-15. According to this verse, what makes us shine?

Do you hear people complaining a lot?

How can we shine out as different from others?

Musical Moment

Sing these words to the tune of "Jesus Loves the Little Children."

Speaking cheerfully to others
Is the godly thing to do.
So don't argue or complain;
Speaking badly is a shame.
Be a star that shines out
Brightly with your cheer.

Digging Deeper

Whom do you know that shines like a star with cheerfulness?

Do you like being around people who complain or argue? What kind of person do you want to be?

Personal Plan

Think about how Jesus lived. Did He ever complain? List some complaints you made this week. Think of ways you can change your attitude to a cheerful one. Copy Philippians 2:14-15 and read it over and over this week.

God's Word in My Life

Timeless Truth

God's Word within me gives peace and direction.

Bible Verse

"Great peace have they who love your law, and nothing can make them stumble." Psalm 119:165

Bible Activity–Paper Plate Pals and Peace!

Before Class

Prepare puppets, using the patterns on pages 95-96; copy the script; and make a stage for presenting the skit.

During Class

Pete: Oh, Patty, look at the dark sky. Look at those branches swaying back and forth. I think I see something! Let's go hide!

Patty: Pete, stop shaking; that's just a shadow. Don't you remember what Mrs. Paulson read from the Bible yesterday? "I will trust and not be afraid. The Lord is my strength and my song!" That's from Isaiah 12:2.

Pete: No, Chris and I were talking in the back row. What was that noise? Patty, I hear someone scratching on the kitchen window. Let's go hide!

Patty: Pete, really, it's OK. That's just a branch my dad is planning to trim tomorrow. It's been rubbing the window recently. Don't you remember the song we sang yesterday about God being our helper? "When I am afraid, I will trust in You."

Pete: I don't remember the song. I hear something again. It's behind the laundry room door. Did you hear it? We have to do something!

Patty: That's Popper, our hamster, on his squeaky exercise wheel. Don't be so afraid of everything. Let me tell you my memory verse for next week, "So do not fear, for I am with you; do not be dismayed, for I am your God. I will strengthen you and help you; I will uphold you with my righteous right hand." Isaiah 41:10. (Pete disappears.)

Patty: Pete, where are you? Did you hear my verse? Pete!

Pete: (in a muffled voice) Patty, I'm behind the couch! Come and tell me your verse again. I've been missing out on some help from God's Word, I guess. I'll come out when I have the verse memorized too.

Patty: Oh, Pete!

Discussion

Who are you more like–Pete or Patty? What helped Patty be brave? What made Pete scared? What can you do to be braver?

Digging Deeper

What do you think Daniel was doing in the lions' den besides praying?

What did Jesus do when Satan tempted Him three times in the desert?

Personal Plan

What Bible verses help you feel peaceful inside? Make a list of some verses you'd like to memorize. Copy Psalm 119:165 and read it over and over this week.

God's Guidance

Timeless Truth

God will be my guide forever.

Bible Verse

"For this God is our God for ever and ever; he will be our guide even to the end." Psalm 48:14

Bible Activity–Maps to the Rescue!

Before Class

Hide prizes around the room to be found with a very simple map. Plan three or four routes to get to each group of prizes.

During Class

After a brief discussion about summer vacations and family outings, hand out the maps and let the children search for the prizes. When all the prizes have been found, discuss what the children learned.

Discussion

Do you use a map when you are going somewhere new with your family?

What is the best map for getting to every new place in life?

Let's read Psalm 48:14. Who is our guide? How does God give us directions?

Digging Deeper

Who guided Moses as he led the children of Israel out of Egypt? What did God use in nature to lead them?

Personal Plan

Where do you keep your guidebook (your Bible)? Is it always handy? Copy Psalm 48:14 and read it over and over this week.

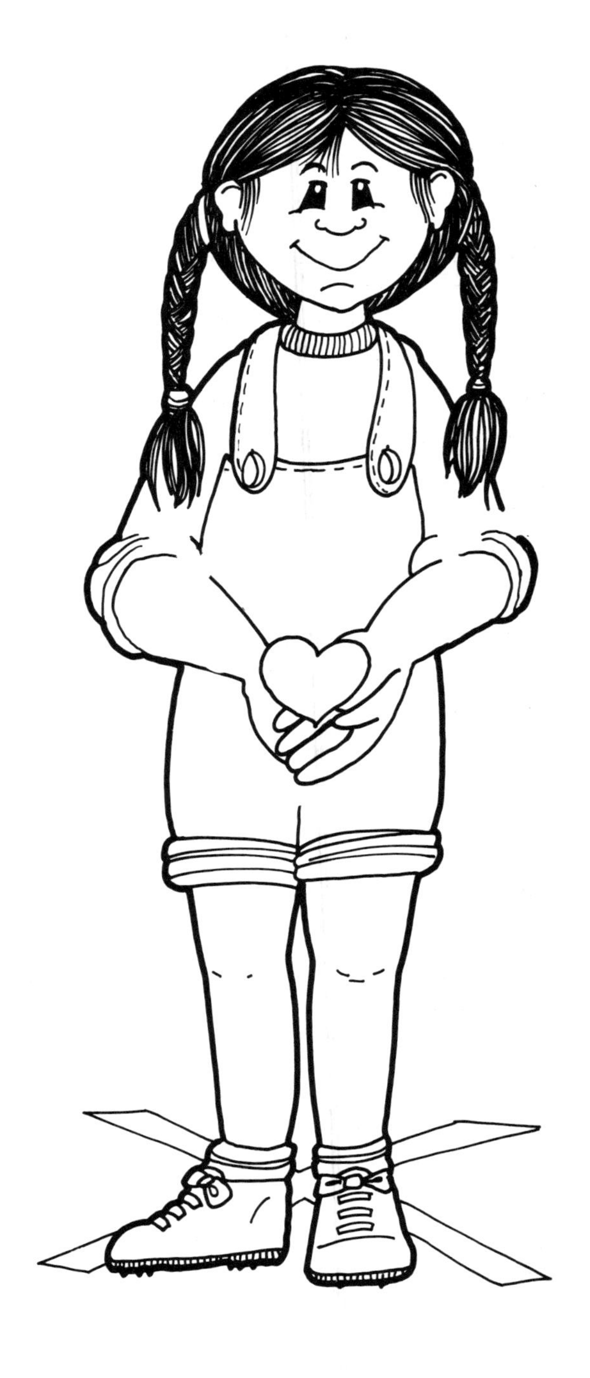

God, the Creator

Timeless Truth

All creatures belong to God.

Bible Verse

"For every animal of the forest is mine, and the cattle on a thousand hills. I know every bird in the mountains, and the creatures of the field are mine."

Psalm 50:10-11

Bible Activity–Creature Feature Celebration

Before Class

Gather these materials:

Stuffed animals (the children may be asked to bring their own)
Small, caged pets (the children may be asked to bring their own)
Picture books of animals
Animal posters
Modeling clay
Paper
Markers or crayons

Display the stuffed animals and pets around the room. Mount the posters on the walls.

Set up two art centers, one with clay and the other with paper and markers.

During Class

Today we're having a Creature Feature Celebration! Use clay or paper and markers to make whatever animal you'd like.

After about ten minutes, allow the children to choose an animal sound they'd like to make. Let them practice. Divide the group according to the animal sounds. Have each group go behind a partition to make their sound one by one. Let the rest of the children vote on the best one by clapping.

Discussion

What is your favorite animal? What animals did you see on your way here today?

What birds did you see? Were they flying?

Let's read Psalm 50:10-11.

Does the Lord know about the animals you saw today?

Does He know about the pets in this room?

Do you think He did a good job in making the animals? Does the animal you made breathe or move?

Digging Deeper

On which day of Creation did God create animals? Read about it in Genesis 1 if you've forgotten. If God knows so much about the animals, how much does He know about you? Since God cares for the animals, how should we treat them?

Personal Plan

Do you ever worry about what clothes to wear or what you'll eat at the next meal? What can you remember this week if you are tempted to worry? Copy Psalm 50:10-11 and read it over and over this week.

Missionaries

Godly Goal

I want to remember the missionaries who are sharing the Gospel in faraway places.

Bible Verse

"Like cold water to a weary soul is good news from a distant land." Proverbs 25:25

Bible Activity–Marching and Munching

Before Class

Have the walls covered with travel posters.

Gather these materials:
Soda crackers
Pretzels
Small paper cups
Pitcher of water
Plastic baggies

During Class

Today we're going on a munching march. We'll march to lots of countries around the world. Let's start marching and munching. Keep it up until I say to stop.

Start your march by leading the children to the first poster, making sure each child has a bag of salty munchies. As you march and munch, tell as much as you can about each country; then march on to the next. Make it a fun march by offering a prize to the best marcher.

When the march is completed, ask the children if they are thirsty.

Give everyone a tiny drink. Then ask if anyone is still thirsty. If so, give each one another drink.

When everyone's thirst is quenched, talk with the children about what a long way missionaries go to tell others about Jesus. Read Proverbs 25:25. Explain that writing a letter to a missionary is like giving him a cool drink of water.

Have everyone write a note and/or draw a picture for a missionary from your church or that your church supports.

Digging Deeper

Look in the back of your Bible for a map showing where Paul traveled on his missionary trips. Do you think he got letters from his friends back home?

List some missionaries you know and where they are serving.

Personal Plan

Which missionary could you adopt to write to every month? Plan to pray for this missionary every night before you go to sleep. Copy Proverbs 25:25 and read it over and over this week.

God, My Best Friend

Godly Goal

I want to walk with God as my best friend.

Bible Verse

"But Noah found favor in the eyes of the Lord . . . . Noah was a righteous man, blameless among the people of his time, and he walked with God." Genesis 6:8-9

Bible Activity–Finger Friends Skit

Before Class

Prepare puppets, using the patterns on pages 95-96; copy the script; and make a stage for presenting the skit.

During Class

Fern: Fred, let's go to the store for a Popsicle™ on the way home from school. It's so hot today!

Fred: That sounds so good! But . . .

Fern: But, what?

Fred: Well, my mom told me to come right home because she wants me to help her in the flower garden.

Fern: Flower garden! Are you kidding? What a boring job! Come on, she won't know you stopped for a little while. I'll even treat you to the Popsicle™–any kind you want.

Fred: Well . . .

Fern: Well what?

Fred: Well, I'd better not!

Fern: Fred, you are such a baby. I don't believe you're the kind of person to be my friend anymore! Good-bye and too bad! (She leaves and Fred walks along in silence for a few moments.)

Fred: God, I only want to do what is right. I want to obey my mom as You command. God, will You be my friend? I feel kind of lonely right now!

Discussion

Have you ever been in a situation like Fred's? Did you feel lonely like Fred? Do you remember Noah? Did he have to do things differently than the people he lived near?

Let's read Genesis 6:8-9. Who became Noah's friend when people laughed at him?

Musical Moment

Sing these words to the tune of "Yankee Doodle."

God wants me to walk with Him.
He'll be my friend forever.

He'll help me learn to do what's right.
He'll never leave me–never!

He's the best friend in the world.
He's the best friend ever.
He will always lead the way
And never leave me–never!

Digging Deeper

What kind of decisions did the following people have to make about doing what was right and keeping their friends happy: Joseph with Potiphar's wife? Daniel and King Darius? Abraham and Lot? David and Jonathan?

Think of people in your life who will be the kind of friends that stick around when you do right. Think about some things in your future that you may have to disagree with your friends about such as drinking, drugs, lying to parents, etc.

Personal Plan

What can you do this week to strengthen your friendship with God? Copy Genesis 6:8-9 and read it over and over this week.

Remembering God's Goodness

Godly Goal

I want to remember what the Lord has done for me.

Bible Verse

"Only be careful, and watch yourselves closely so that you do not forget the things your eyes have seen or let them slip from your heart as long as you live. Teach them to your children and to their children after them." Deuteronomy 4:9

Bible Activity–Tricky Trays

Before Class

Take several small trays to class. Also take enough miscellaneous items, such as hairbows, pens, combs, toothbrushes, toothpicks, mugs, etc., to be divided up and placed in paper bags for the children in groups. Each child should also have paper to write on.

During Class

Divide the children into groups of two to four, depending on the number of trays available. Give each group a tray and eight to ten of the small items. Have one person start out as the "tricky tray leader." That person takes five to eight items from the bag with his back to the others in the group (or the others can cover their eyes).

When the teacher calls, "Start," the other group members look at the things on the tray. After ten seconds the teacher calls, "Stop." The tray should be covered or placed completely out of sight.

Everyone but the "tricky tray leader" writes down all the things he can remember seeing on the tray. After a minute or so the teacher calls for pencils to be put down, and the tray is returned for checking.

Let each person in the groups have a turn at being leader. Before each new turn, have the groups trade bags of tray items.

For added excitement, keep track of which group or person does best at remembering.

When the game is over, ask some questions. Do you have a good memory? Would this game be easier if you had longer to look at the things on the tray? Would it be easier if you were all alone so you could concentrate more easily? Would it be easier if you could compare lists with one another?

Let's read Deuteronomy 4:9. God told the children of Israel not to forget the way He had taken care of them. What has the Lord done for you? What blessings has He given you?

Do you take time regularly to thank Him when you are alone and quiet? Would it help you remember to thank Him if you talked to others about all He has done?

Digging Deeper

What are some of the things the children of Israel could be thankful for after they left Egypt?

What do you think Daniel thanked God for when he prayed?

What do you think the disciples thanked God for after Jesus appeared to them after His resurrection?

Personal Plan

Make a list of things you don't want to forget that God has done for you. Copy Deuteronomy 4:9 and read it over and over this week.

Winning with God

Timeless Truth

Don't trust in your own strength or victories; trust in God.

Bible Verse

"Some trust in chariots and some in horses, but we trust in the name of the LORD our God." Psalm 20:7

Bible Activity–Pencil Pulling

Before Class

Gather these materials:

A car pattern from page 92 for each child

Pencils

String or yarn (36" long piece for each child)

Tape

During Class

Give each child a pencil, a 36" piece of yarn, and a car pattern. Have the child cut out the car and attach yarn to it with tape. The other end of the yarn should be taped to the middle of the pencil.

The object of the game is to race the car, rolling up the yarn on the pencil, pulling the pattern toward you. Start the race with the yarn stretched out the same length from each pencil.

Have several races to see if the children can improve. They may even want to race the clock instead of one another.

Discussion

Do you feel better about yourself when you win a race or get the highest grade? Does God love people who win and get good grades more than people who lose and get bad grades?

God wants us to do our best, but He also wants us to realize that all our talents and abilities are from Him. He wants us to trust Him for everything and to give Him honor.

Digging Deeper

Name some Bible characters who failed. (For example, Peter denied Jesus.) What is their standing before God even with their past failures?

Think of schoolmates whom you would not call winners. Does God love them as much as He loves winners?

Personal Plan

Whom can you encourage this week who isn't a regular winner in sports or in academics? Can you tell him or her not to trust in strength or victories but to trust in God? Copy Psalm 20:7 and read it over and over this week.

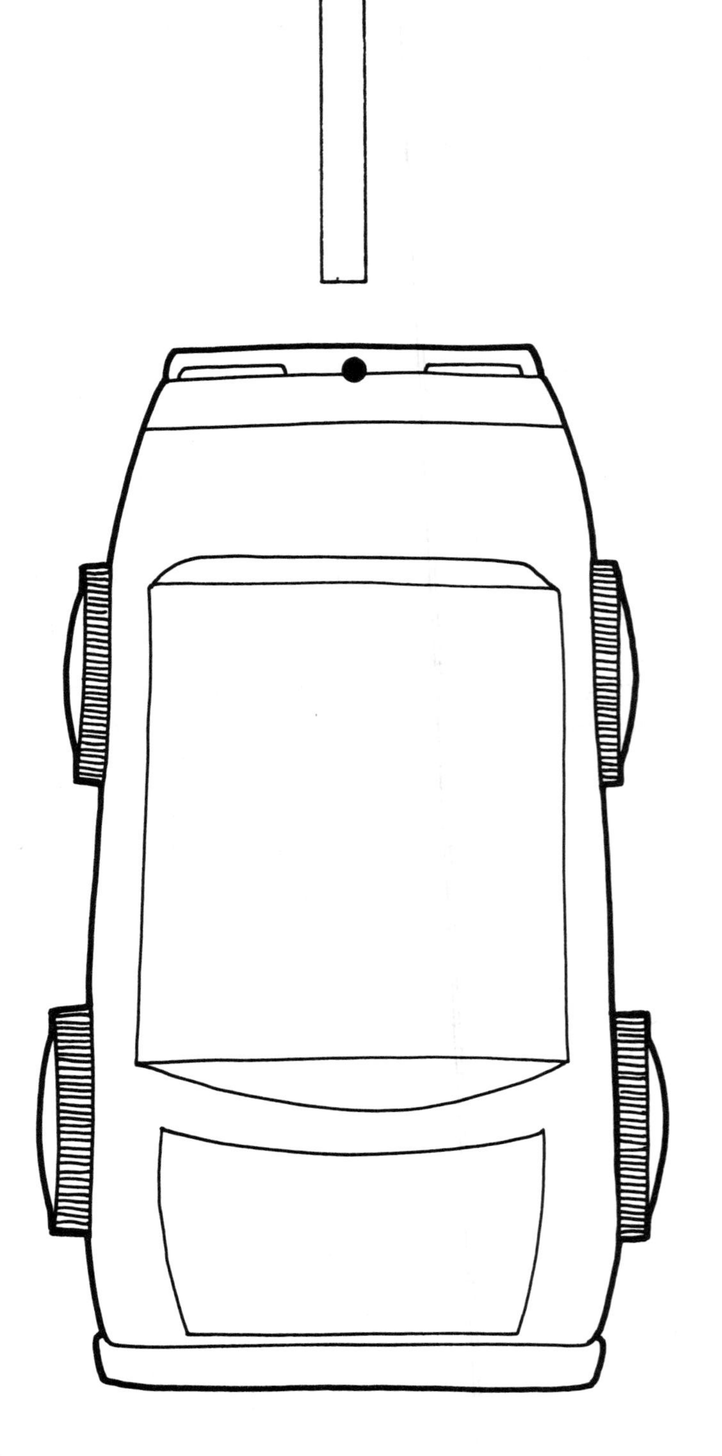

Following God

Godly Goal

I want to follow God wholeheartedly. (Valentine's Day)

Bible Verse

". . . Caleb has a different spirit and follows me wholeheartedly."

Numbers 14:24a

Bible Activity–Undone Fun!

Before Class

Prepare the following items, one for each group:

Separate some sandwich cookies.

Remove a few pieces from some fifteen- to thirty-piece puzzles.

Tape some favorite songs that the children will know, but stop just before the ends of the songs.

Print the Bible verse above on cards, one word per card. Leave one word out. Put the cards in an envelope.

During Class

Divide the children into teams and give each team a puzzle to put together. Give the signal for them to begin; then see how long it takes them to realize there are pieces missing. Apologize and collect the puzzles.

Start playing the music and tell the children that they will be able to have a snack while they listen. Give them each a sandwich cookie without the top half. Listen to their responses. Apologize again.

Give each group an envelope of Bible verse cards and have them use their Bibles to put the verse together. Apologize again as they tell you a piece is missing.

Discussion

What has gone wrong today? What things were missing? Did you get a little frustrated?

Let's try using all the envelopes to see if we can put one whole verse together.

After you put the verse together, read it aloud.

Do you ever do things in a halfhearted way? Do you ever clean your room, but leave a few things undone? Do you ever help clean the kitchen, but leave a few crumbs on the counter?

Do you sometimes do only part of the things that would please God? What does it mean to follow God wholeheartedly?

Let's eat some whole cookies and finish our whole puzzles.

Digging Deeper

Whom can you think of in the Bible besides Caleb who followed God wholeheartedly? Whom do you know who follows God wholeheartedly? Will God help you follow wholeheartedly?

Personal Plan

List some ways you have not followed God wholeheartedly. What are some things you want to change this week? Copy Numbers 14:24a and read it over and over this week.

Boy Puppet Pattern

1. Cut out the pattern.
2. Trace two on felt or other fabric.
3. Sew together, leaving the bottom open.

Girl Puppet Pattern

1. Cut out the pattern.
2. Trace two on felt or other fabric.
3. Sew together, leaving the bottom open.